THE
of the
BIBLE

An Illustrated Guide to the Holy Land, Its People, and Its History

Abingdon Press
Nashville

Thank you for visiting the Holy Land with us. Since 1974, we have designed Holy Land programs to provide firsthand knowledge of the lands, history, culture, and peoples of this important region—past and present. Our travel experiences not only visit sites you have read about in the Bible but also include interaction with residents, local authorities, and scholars.

We are happy to provide you with *The Land of the Bible: An Illustrated Guide to the Holy Land, Its People, and Its History*. Author Lamontte M. Luker has traveled with us for many years and is Dean of the Jerusalem Center for Biblical Studies. JCBS serves professors and students of colleges, universities, and seminaries by combining in-depth lectures with extensive field trips. This guide provides comprehensive and practical insights that will help you before and during your trip to the Holy Land. It is also a great resource to use after you travel for your everyday Bible reading and study.

All of us pray that your Holy Land experience will bring the Bible to life, deepen your faith, energize your ministry, and change your life.

Sincerely,

James Ridgway
President & CEO
Educational Opportunities

Haifa, 6 September 2013

Dear Brother Lamontte Luker,

You have been enough times in the Holy Land. You immersed yourself reconnecting back the two thousand years of an exciting story. Indeed the man you write about, Jesus Christ, the places you introduce so eloquently for a large yet undetermined number of people, that Man is risen, and we have His Empty Tomb. It seems that Galilee, which is considered by many scholars and spiritual men and women to be the fifth Gospel, has deeply impacted your spiritual experience. With this book you yearn to share your experience with as many people as possible. I myself being another man from Galilee, I thank God for your long and fruitful experience and for the courage you had to make time and share with others what the Lord allowed you to experience.

You are always invited back again to continue being in touch with the Living Stones, the Local Palestinian Christians who continue to be most faithful to their own Compatriot and their outstanding Champion Jesus Christ the Savior.

Yours sincerely,

Abuna Elias Chacour
Melkite Catholic Archbishop of Galilee

THE LAND OF THE BIBLE: AN ILLUSTRATED GUIDE
TO THE HOLY LAND, ITS PEOPLE, AND ITS HISTORY

Copyright © 2019 by Abingdon Press

ISBN 978-1-5018-9231-8

Scripture quotations are from the Common English Bible. Copyright © 2011 by the Common English Bible. All rights reserved. Used by permission. www.CommonEnglishBible.com.

All photographs are from the author's private collection. © Lamontte M. Luker

Maps of Israel on pp. 7 and 102 and map of Egypt on p. 103 courtesy Stephen Robles and Lamontte M. Luker.

20 21 22 23 24 25 26 27 28— 10 9 8 7 6 5 4 3 2

MANUFACTURED IN THE USA

Contents

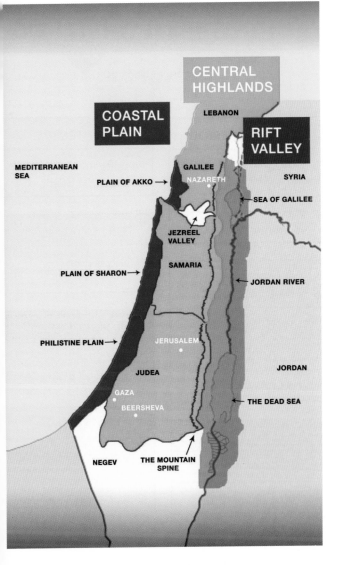

CENTRAL
HIGHLANDS

COASTAL
PLAIN

LEBANON

RIFT
VALLEY

MEDITERRANEAN
SEA

GALILEE

← PLAIN OF AKKO →   NAZARETH

SYRIA

← SEA OF GALILEE

JEZREEL
VALLEY

SAMARIA

← PLAIN OF SHARON →

← JORDAN RIVER

JERUSALEM

← PHILISTINE PLAIN →

JUDEA

JORDAN

GAZA

BEERSHEVA

← THE DEAD SEA

NEGEV   THE MOUNTAIN
SPINE

ISRAEL TIMELINE

(Dates are beginnings)

MODERN PERIOD

Israel: 1948 CE

British: 1917 CE

Ottoman: 1516 CE

ISLAM & MIDDLE AGES

Mamluk: 1291 CE

Crusader: 1099 CE

Muslim: 638 CE

MISHNAH & TALMUD

Byzantine: 324 CE

Roman: 63 BCE

FIRST TEMPLE

Israelite (Iron Age 2–3): 1004 BCE

THE SETTLEMENT

Judges (Iron Age 1): 1200 BCE

IN EGYPT

Canaanite (Bronze Age): 3600 BCE

OLD AGES

Chalcolithic: 5800 BCE

Stone Age: before 5800 BCE

Introduction

You are engaged in a great adventure. The Holy Land evokes mystery and significance for the faithful who travel there. Experiencing the Holy Land brings to life the names and people you've only read about, and even the best-informed and most enthusiastic pilgrims need a guide as they travel to see the sites for themselves. As the geographic heart and soul of Judaism, Islam, and Christianity, the Holy Land holds immense significance for its millions of visitors each year. But the meaning of the Holy Land for each person is unique.

This guide to the Holy Land gives historical background and archaeological descriptions wedded to the biblical text. It is meant to be a resource not just for a casual vacation or tour, but for spiritual formation. It is meant to help you understand both what you see and the undercurrents of what you may not see. It will help you understand the peoples of long ago, but also how people live in the Holy Land today.

Packed with the latest information, this book will introduce you to popular and less-familiar sites, such as Nazareth and the Basilica of the Annunciation, Bethlehem, the Church of the Nativity, the Herodium, the Mount of Olives, the Old City of Jerusalem, Wadi Kelt, Mount Sinai, the Church of the Holy Sepulcher, the Temple Mount, the traditional tomb of King David (and another site that might be his actual tomb), the traditional house of Caiaphas the high priest (and its more probable historical location), the Shrine of the Book, Herod's Antonio Fortress, Golgotha, Bethany, the tomb of Lazarus, Gethsemane, and many others. Each entry explains the history and topography of the site, as well as its function and significance as it is linked to the relevant biblical passages.

As a professor of religion and a student of archaeology, I have lived and studied in the Holy Land for thirty years, walking the Bible with countless tour groups, students, and pilgrims. I can help you put together the puzzle pieces of history, religion, and current events as you use this guide to immerse yourself in the land and its people.

My hope is that this book will not only inform you but help you better understand your faith.

Archaeology in Israel

Archaeology in Israel is a controversial and political topic. When the art and science of archaeology was being birthed at the end of the nineteenth and beginning of the twentieth centuries CE, the assumption was that one could use the Bible as an archaeological map. As the practice of archaeology evolved, however, scholars began to take into account that the Bible is not only a historical book but also a theological book. By the end of the last century, the pendulum had swung entirely the other way, to the extent that some scholars refused to use the Bible as an archaeological guide at all. Only what got dug up was considered historically relevant anymore.

The latter approach only considers carbon dating and archaeological artifacts found *in situ* as dependable evidence. This has spawned two major schools of thought. Those who embrace the so-called "High Chronology" basically follow the biblical witness whenever there is archaeological evidence for support. Those who champion the so-called "Low Chronology," on the other hand, lower the biblical dates by a century. For example, the building projects of David and Solomon (tenth century BCE) are moved to Omri and Ahab in the ninth century BCE. To make matters more complicated, while the term "biblical archaeology" is a relatively neutral term in America, in Israel it connotes a fundamentalism associated with the ultra-Orthodox.

Over the years, I have followed the debates closely and believe that, in general, the evidence both from carbon dating and in situ data supports the High Chronology. In dialogue with my colleagues in the United States and Israel, this is the position I follow in this book.

Historical Context

The Christian Church has traditionally referred to dates after the year zero as Anno Domini (AD), "in the year of the Lord (Jesus)," and the years before zero as Before Christ (BC). Since Christians, Jews, and Muslims study the Holy Land together in the twenty-first century, an ecumenical terminology can also be used: After the year zero is the Common Era (CE), and before the year zero is Before the Common Era (BCE).

The stories of the patriarchs Abraham, Isaac, and Jacob, and their families (Genesis 12–50), came from the middle Bronze Age (2000–1550 BCE). The Israelite period that roughly includes the time of Joshua until the Babylonian exile (1200–586 BCE) is the Iron Age. The time from Solomon in the tenth century to the end of the Iron Age is also referred to as the First Temple period.

When the Jews returned from the Babylonian exile, they were not allowed to reestablish the monarchy during the Persian period (538–332 BCE) and instead developed a hierocracy (a rule of the high priest) in the province of Yehud. The Temple in Jerusalem was rebuilt ca. 516 BCE, and the span of time from that year until the Temple's destruction in 70 CE is known as the Second Temple period.

Alexander the Great initiated the Hellenistic period (332–63 BCE). Then, with Pompey's conquest came the Roman period (63 BCE–324 CE). Within the Roman period, historians distinguish two eras. There was a period of Jewish independence under the rule of the Hasmonean family (167–40 BCE); and there was the rule of King Herod (37–4 BCE).

The Byzantine (Christian) period is specified as 324–640 CE, followed by the first Muslim period in 640–1099. The Crusaders ruled the Holy Land from 1099 to 1291, after which time the Muslims regained control under the leadership of the Egyptian Mamluks (1291–1517). The Ottoman Turks ruled the Holy Land from 1517 to 1918 (World War I), during which time it was deforested to make way for and to build their steam-engine railways and because of the property tax on trees.[1] The period of the British Mandate lasted until just after the end of World War II (1918–1948).

Many readers will be coming to the Holy Land not only for an archaeological experience or as a pilgrim but also for the cross-cultural experience that the Holy Land has to offer. However, the political and cultural situation is very difficult to understand for anyone who has not lived here. When you begin the trip, you may have opinions about the politics

> **Pilgrims come to the Holy Land for the archaeological and the cross-cultural experiences.**

and culture of the Holy Land, but you will probably go home confused because the situation is gray, not black and white.

The only people ever to have had a nation here were biblical Israel. Before them were Canaanite city-states under Egyptian rule, and from 70 to 1948 CE, no nation emerged under the hegemony of various foreign empires. Jews never stopped living in the Holy Land. Some of them, though not all, became Christians in the first centuries of the Common Era. In the seventh century, Muslims established a presence in the land and added another religion to the mix: Jews, Christians, and Muslims living together in one land. As Archbishop Elias Chacour of Galilee is fond of saying, "We Christians, Jews, and Muslims don't have to learn how to live together; we just have to remember how we used to live together." Chacour's book, *Blood Brothers* (Grand Rapids, MI: Zondervan, 1984), is a great thing to read before beginning your study or pilgrimage in Israel. The following books are also recommended:

- Bruce Feiler, *Abraham: A Journey to the Heart of Three Faiths* (New York: HarperCollins, 2002)

- Larry Collins and Dominique Lapierre, *O Jerusalem!* (New York: Simon and Schuster, 1972), a history of the Israeli war for independence, which Arabs call "The Disaster"

- Naim Stifan Ateek, *Justice, and Only Justice: A Palestinian Theology of Liberation* (Mary Knoll, NY: Orbis, 1989)

- Amy Dockser Marcus, *Jerusalem 1913: The Origins of the Arab-Israeli Conflict* (New York: Penguin, 2007)

- Adrian Wolff, *A Chronology of Israel: A Complete History from Biblical to Modern Times with Photographs and Maps,* 2nd ed. (Adrian Wolff, 2010), a detailed historical textbook from Abraham to the present, as seen by the Israeli author

Although there are many, many dates and events that have contributed to the current situation in the Holy Land, these events' significance will continue to change and develop; therefore, only the most important instances follow. In an attempt to offer a solution to Jews, Christians, and Muslims living in the same land, the United Nations partitioned the area according to population density in 1947. The Jews accepted the partition; the Arabs did not. War broke out. The Jews won and acquired more land in the process. The 1948 armistice allotted the central part of the Holy Land, biblical Judea and Samaria, to the governance of the Hashemite Kingdom of Jordan (which itself was a creation of British sovereignty). So this was the territory of Jordan that lay west of the Jordan River (the "West Bank"). The 1967 Six-Day War ended with Israel occupying Judea and Samaria, the West Bank. The 1973 Yom Kippur War maintained the status quo.

An important definition is required here. *Palestinian* refers to an Arab, Christian or Muslim, who lives in the Holy Land. Many Christian Arabs are descendants of Jesus' disciples and followers. Palestinians who live in Israel are citizens of Israel. To quote Archbishop Elias Chacour again, "I am an Arab, Palestinian, Christian, Israeli." Now, go figure.

Professors, pastors, and tour leaders who read this book will often have their own cross-cultural contacts, but here are a few others that you may find helpful:

- Pilgrims of Ibillin: www.pilgrimsofibillin.org
- International Center of Bethlehem: www.annadwa.org/Con_Speeches.htm
- Augusta Victoria Hospital Jerusalem: www.lwfjerusalem.org/wp/
- Bob Lang, former spokesman for the YESHA council and leader in the Jewish neighborhood of Efrat near Bethlehem: <bblang@zahav.net.il>
- Sabeel: www.sabeel.org

Geographical Overview

A map is provided with this introduction. It can be fleshed out by reading the description of Israel's topography in the section on Gezer ("Interesting Places to See in the Shefela"). In the middle of this book is a larger map showing the places discussed herein.

Individual regional explanations are to be found within the articles in each section.

- There is no one best way to organize your tour of the Holy Land. This book is arranged as follows:

- Northern Coast, Sharon Plain

- Galilee

- Samaria

- Judea

- Central and Southern Negev

- Shefela

- Southern Coast, Philistine Plain

Gezer is a good place to begin or end with for a geographical overview, but this can be accomplished from other places as well, such as Mount Carmel, Megiddo, the Mount of Olives, or the Herodium.

You will notice the Hebrew word *tel* in front of a lot of place-names in the Holy Land. This is an archaeological term that refers to an artificial conical mound created by an ancient city's destruction and subsequent rebuilding many times over the centuries.

Practical Information

The Israel National Park Authority sells a ticket for all national parks at a discounted rate (see www.parks.org.il). Note that the national parks close at 4 p.m. in winter and 5 p.m. in summer. Parks also close one hour earlier on Fridays and holiday eves, and many lock their gates one hour before closing time. Always ask for the national park brochure at the entrance kiosk of each park you visit.

Churches in the Holy Land normally are closed between noon and 2 p.m., but there are exceptions. See the schedule at the Christian Information Center website (www.cicts.org), or visit their office at Jaffa Gate, Old City, Jerusalem.

In general, dress informally and practically, with layers you can put on or take off. The Middle East is a modest culture, so shoulders and knees must be covered when visiting holy places. Good walking shoes are a must. Try to avoid checking into an Israeli hotel or kibbutz (a communal settlement) on Saturday because the sabbath custom of late checkout may delay your check-in. This applies to Jewish holidays as well, when rates are usually higher.

If you are with a group, you will need a competent organization to help you with travel plans. A very good one is the Jerusalem Center for Biblical Studies (phone: 888-431-7902; website: www. jcbs.org). The following description is quoted from their web page:

> The Jerusalem Center for Biblical Studies began in 1980 through the inspiration of Dr. Jim Ridgway, founder and President of Educational Opportunities, Inc., a non-profit Christian travel ministry located in Lakeland, Florida. The original purpose was to offer pastors travel/study programs to Israel, Palestine, Jordan, Egypt, Turkey, Greece and Rome for enrichment of their ministry. These programs provided active academic learning within a geographic, cultural, archaeological and Biblical context.

> The Center later made their travel/study programs available to church laity and to the academic community including colleges, universities, seminaries, and graduate schools. Many academic leaders have partnered with JCBS to give their students exciting educational experiences.

Abbreviations

ABD—Anchor Bible Dictionary
BAR—Biblical Archaeology Review
JPS Tanakh—(The) New Jewish Publication Society of America Tanakh
NEA—Near Eastern Archaeology
NEAEHL—(The) New Encyclopedia of Archaeological Excavations in the Holy Land
NIDB—New Interpreter's Dictionary of the Bible
MDB—Mercer Dictionary of the Bible

Northern Coast, Sharon Plain

⭐ **Caesarea (National Park)**

*Also known as: Caesarea Maritime
(to distinguish from Caesarea Philippi)*

Located on the Mediterranean coast between Tel Aviv and Haifa, Caesarea (previously Strato's Tower) was a gift to Herod the Great (37–4 BCE) from his patron Augustus Caesar (hence its name) in 30 BCE. The new city was constructed by Herod in only twelve years (22–10 BCE).

Enter at the ticket gate nearest the theater (this southern entrance to the park is the road from the Caesarea Interchange) and ask when the next movie in English is showing. Then proceed straight ahead into the site (restrooms are

Aqueducts of Caesarea

on the right) to the large white building housing a commendable media presentation on the history of Caesarea. This serves as an excellent introduction to the site. Then backtrack to Herod's theater (directly across from the restrooms).

The theater seated four thousand people, and the Roman rule of thumb was that there should be a theater seat for each ten residents of the city, suggesting that Herod's Caesarea had a population of about forty thousand people. As is obvious, except for the first row, most of the seats have been restored, and the current theater is used for concerts and productions throughout the warmer months. Similarly, only a few of the original marble pavements are extant in the orchestra floor. The stage is wood, as it would have been in Herod's time, with alternating square and circular niches for decorative statuary. Behind the stage was an elaborate backdrop of granite pillars (imported from Egypt or Asia Minor, as granite is not indigenous to Israel) to aid in sound projection, and many of these can be seen in the archaeological park beyond the theater toward the sea. Beneath the stage are the rooms for the performers, which can be visited via the staircases. The acoustics are perfect, and this is a good place to seat your group while someone volunteers to sing from the stage.

> **Make sure to check out the theater's perfect acoustics.**

There was no Judaism at the time of Jesus. There were various Jewish sects, each claiming to be the true heir to Israel's history and scriptures: Sadducees, Pharisees, Essenes, Zealots, Hellenists, baptizers; and later the *Notsrim* (or Nazarenes; Matthew 2:23), Jews who believed that a certain itinerant rabbi from Nazareth was executed by the Romans but raised by God from the dead and is the Messiah who is ushering in the fulfillment of God's kingdom. All these groups were exclusively Jewish.

Enter Cornelius at Caesarea (Acts 10). Cornelius was a "God-fearer," one of a fairly large number of Gentiles in the first century who had become disenchanted with the Greco-Roman myths. These God-fearers were intrigued by the monotheism of the Jews and attended synagogue, but they did not convert for obvious social, dietary, and physical reasons. This Cornelius wanted to join the Notsrim, which presented the Jesus movement with a dilemma: Cornelius was not Jewish. Had not Jesus himself said, "Don't go among the Gentiles. . . . Go instead to the lost sheep, the people of Israel" (Matthew 10:5-6)?

So the Notsrim sought the advice of Peter, who was staying farther south on the coast at Jaffa. Curiously, Peter had just received

> See a replica of the only object to mention Pontius Pilate by name.

a vision of a tablecloth full of nonkosher food with the instruction to eat, by which Peter began to become aware that God was doing something new with this Jesus movement. So he traveled to Caesarea and became convinced that this "something new" was nothing less than the fulfillment of God's promise to Abraham and Sarah: that God would make of them a nation, give them a land, and that through them the Gentiles would be blessed by coming to know the world's only true God (Genesis 12:1-3). The Jesus movement provided Cornelius and the minions of other God-fearers around the Mediterranean with a way to embrace monotheism without becoming Jewish. And Christianity, as a religion of Jews and Gentiles who know and worship the God of Abraham and Sarah, became a reality starting right there in Caesarea.

Exit the theater behind the stage and follow the path through the archaeological garden and the breach in the wall of an Umayyad fortress, turning left to Herod's palace (praetorium) which became the palace of the Roman procurator (prefect) in 6 CE. You will find yourself in the upper courtyard of the two-tiered palace. In the center is a replica of the limestone slab that is the only object from the first century mentioning Pontius Pilate (26–36 CE). It reads "[building in honor of] Tiberius . . . [Pon]tius Pilate . . . [Praef]ect of Judea."[2] Archaeologists discovered this dedication in the theater, but it must have adorned a temple in Caesarea that Pilate built to honor Tiberius Caesar.

Walk to the western edge of the courtyard and look down to the sea below to view the remains of the lower tier of the palace: a rectangular swimming pool was surrounded by two-story living quarters. The mosaic floors of the triclinium (dining room) and an adjacent room are visible between the pool and where you are standing.

> Paul appeared before Roman procurators and the Jewish king in the audience hall.

Continue walking around the courtyard of the upper palace to the northern side and you will come to a clearly marked audience hall, which is likely where Paul argued his defense before Roman procurators Felix and Festus and Jewish king Agrippa II during his imprisonment here at the praetorium for more than two years (59–62 CE; Acts 23:33–25:27). Had Paul not appealed to Caesar, it appears he would have been set free, but instead he sailed for Rome, where he lived under house arrest, preaching the gospel, from 62 to 64 (Acts 28:30–31). According to Christian tradition, he was martyred sometime after the fire of Rome (64 CE) during Nero's persecution of Christians.

Exit the palace courtyard at the eastern end, where you originally entered, and look to the left to see Herod's large oval amphitheater. You will find a path through the excavations to take you down to its floor. Its dimensions are roughly 950 x 165 feet, and there were twelve rows of seats for about ten thousand spectators. It was used for races (see the starting gates at the north end near the reconstructed chariot) and athletic events. Herod held celebratory games here in 11 BCE to inaugurate his new city. This unusually long and narrow structure was usurped by a hippodrome built in the second century CE, and by a smaller amphitheater constructed in the far northeast portion of the city during the third century.

If time is short, proceed directly to the Crusader city. If time allows, wander to the east to view the Byzantine bathhouse constructed after the amphitheater had ceased to function. Then continue north to what was probably the Herodian *cardo* (the essential north-south road in a Roman town) but now appears in its Byzantine version, boasting of an archive building with quotations from Paul to encourage the payment of taxes (Romans 13:3)! Continue walking toward the entrance of the Crusader city to pass a series of Roman warehouses, one of which was made a Mithraeum—a temple to the god Mithras, who is often identified with the sun—in which sunlight strikes the altar (see the ceiling) at noon on the summer solstice (June 21).

Enter the Crusader city, which had a population of about twelve thousand. That's less than one-third the size of Herod's Caesarea and roughly one-eighth the size of the Byzantine city. The dry moat and originally ten-meter wall you are passing date to King Louis IX of France (1214–70 CE). The grassy lawn before you represents the eastern extent of the inner harbor, and above the reeds are Roman warehouses. You may walk to the water. The western extent of Herod's harbor was approximately the same as the current harbor, which is now adorned by a Crusader citadel, a mosque, and modern restaurants and shops. Aerial photographs, underwater excavation, and a submerged tower reveal the outer harbor to have extended about sixty-five feet from the shore. Herod created this artificial harbor (the natural harbor in biblical times was Jaffa) by filling barges with stones and cement until they sank into place. However, eventually nature took its toll, and this feat of Roman engineering lasted a mere century before sinking into the sea.

Northern Coast, Sharon Plain

Move toward the exit on the northeast corner of the Crusader city, passing the Roman nymphaeum (public fountain), across from which are restrooms (that should be utilized, since there are none at the aqueducts, where you are going next). Just before you get to the northeastern gate, you may turn right if time allows. This will lead you down the Crusader covered street to Herod's temple, dedicated to Augustus. This structure subsequently became an octagonal Byzantine church (sixth century CE), a mosque, and finally the triple-apsed Crusader Cathedral of St. Peter. Retrace your steps back to the magnificent Crusader vaulted ceiling gate, which serves as the park's exit.

The road to Or Akiva will take your vehicle to the aqueducts. The first turn on the right leads to a modern arch, from which Hadrian's hippodrome can be viewed. However, the best way to reach it is by going back toward the Crusader city a hundred yards and taking the dirt road on foot.

As the city of Caesarea grew, it needed more and more water. The aqueduct in front of you as you arrive at the parking lot originally reached five miles northeast to the Shuni springs and was later extended into Nahal Tanninim. There are three water channels on top of it. The one closest to the parking lot was built by a first-century Roman procurator. The one

Romans and later empires built and rebuilt the aqueducts.

facing the sea was built by Hadrian. The clay pipe is Byzantine. Anyone feeling adventurous can explore another fourth-century aqueduct by way of a narrow path at the northeast corner of the parking lot.

Caesarea was truly one of the Holy Land's most significant cities. Conflict between Gentiles and Jews here erupted into the First Jewish Revolt of 66–70 CE, and Roman general Vespasian was declared Caesar here in 69 CE. Rabbi Akiva and other Jewish leaders of the Second Jewish Revolt (132–135 CE) were tortured and killed by the Romans here; and in 306 CE, Emperor Maximinus executed Christian martyrs in the Roman (second) amphitheater. Nonetheless, Caesarea became a renowned center of Jewish learning in the third and fourth centuries CE and was the home of the great Christian scholar Origen from 231 to 250 CE. By the time church historian and biblical geographer Eusebius became Bishop of Caesarea in 314 CE, only Alexandria could boast a larger library.

Statue of Elijah at Muhraka, Mount Carmel

Mount Carmel

Crowning Israel's modern Mediterranean harbor (the biblical one was Jaffa; Herod's was Caesarea) is Haifa, a cosmopolitan and multicultural city atop which sits the University of Haifa—the only university in Israel in which the percentage of

Arab students is equal to the percentage of the Arab population of Israel. Haifa is the center of the Baha'i religion with its impressive shrine and gardens. The mountain is also home to Druze citizens, as well as a messianic Jewish community (see www.carmel-assembly.org.il). Along its

> **Elijah's famous contest with the 450 prophets of Baal was on Mount Carmel.**

highest ridge is Muhraqa (see www.muhraqa.org), the Carmelite monastery that commemorates Elijah's famous contest with the 450 prophets of Baal (1 Kings 18).

Northernmost Coast

Akko on the horizon across the Haifa harbor.

Akko
Also known as Acre

Most groups will not have this luxury, but if you can visit north of Haifa, the Crusader city of Akko (visible from the Haifa overlook at Stella Maris) is worth it. However, you'll want to note that it is "way up there" in terms of travel time. Park outside the Old City and begin at the Visitors' Center to get maps and directions (see www.akko.org.il/en/). The restaurants along the shore specialize in alfresco dining, including shellfish, which is not otherwise available in Israel except in Haifa, Tel Aviv, and, of course, Arab restaurants.

Rosh Hanikra

Really off the beaten path is Rosh Hanikra on the Lebanese border. Board the cable car that descends from the chalk cliffs to the grottoes on the Mediterranean Sea below. The White Cliffs of Dover have nothing on this location!

Rosh Hanikra

NOTES

NOTES

Galilee

Canaanite shrine

Megiddo (National Park)

Begin in the small museum at the model of ninth-century BCE Megiddo (from the time of Kings Omri and Ahab). In two portions of the model, earlier Canaanite levels are visible if you press the hydraulic buttons.

Megiddo has a long and varied history indeed, dating from the fourth millennium BCE. Different archaeological excavations since 1903 have revealed at least twenty cities buried here, one on top of the other. It is positioned on a hill overlooking the juncture of the Via Maris and the Jezreel Valley, the major military and mercantile passages of the Holy Land. Thus it is not surprising that

Megiddo is the location of the first major battle recorded in history. As immortalized in the Karnak Temple, Pharaoh Thutmose III soundly defeated the city-state and secured Canaan within the realm of the Egyptian Empire (1468 BCE). About a century later, Megiddo's King Biridiya wrote letters to Pharaoh Akhenaten. These written accounts, along with archaeological finds, attest to the city's might and bounty.

Megiddo remained a Canaanite city during the tribal confederacy (Judges 1:27), but was probably taken by David and then fortified by Solomon (1 Kings 9:15) with a casemate wall and gate. However, Pharaoh Shishak (Shoshenq I) destroyed Solomon's city in 925 BCE, as attested by his inscriptions both at the Karnak Temple and on a stele discovered at Megiddo. It was rebuilt on a grander scale by the monarchy of the Northern Kingdom of Israel, as seen in the model before you.

After studying the model and reviewing this history, proceed to the video room for a short video, and then exit the back door to begin walking the tel.

The current path enters the site through the sixteenth-century BCE Canaanite gate, but before entering, look to your left to an earlier path. These steps led to a post-Solomonic water system, but just above them you can see the right half of Solomon's outer gate. After passing through the Canaanite gate, you will arrive at the foundations of the left half of Solomon's inner three-chambered gate, and just a bit farther up the path is a palace built concurrently with the gate.

Continue up all the way to the southeast edge of the tel to the Canaanite sacred precinct used throughout the third millennium BCE. The long, narrow temple immediately in front of you is similar to the one at En Gedi (ca. 3000 BCE). The central round altar (ca. 2500 BCE) reminds us of a stipulation in an early Israelite collection of laws often called the Covenant Code (Exodus 20:22–23:33): "Don't climb onto my altar using steps: then your genitals won't be exposed by doing so" (Exodus 20:26). This was evidently a proscription against Canaanite fertility worship and its practices. As you can see, eventually a two-room temple was attached to the round altar, and subsequently two more temples were built just beyond it.

Walk a few steps to the eastern edge of the tel to study the panorama. Before you is the vast Jezreel Valley. Of all the battles

Galilee

that took place in the expanse of this valley, none is more famous than the one between some of the Israelite tribes led by Deborah and Barak and the region's Canaanite city-states led by Sisera. "Deborah's song" (Judges 5), the oldest poem in the Bible, celebrates the

> "Deborah's Song" (Judges 5) is the oldest poem in the Bible.

improbable victory of the Israelites over the Canaanite forces.

Deborah gathered the tribes willing to participate on Mount Tabor. Sisera, who dwelt in Harosheth-ha-goiim (Judges 4:2-8), the plain just east of Megiddo and just below where you are standing, set up his chariot camp there. Flowing in between the two is the Kishon River. What happened next was viewed by the Israelites as little short of a miracle: it rained. The Kishon flooded the plain (as still happens today in a heavy rain), the Canaanite chariots became stuck in the mud, and the Israelites descended upon Sisera's helpless army from Mount Tabor. Sisera sought to save himself by escaping to the east of Mount Tabor, seeking refuge in the tent of Jael the Kenite (Midianite). But Jael displayed an allegiance to Deborah by assassinating Sisera, and an emerging Israel was saved by the heroic actions of two women.

Backtrack a bit, but stay to the left until you come to a grain silo with a pair of stairs. Just a bit farther is a series of rectangular buildings, one of which is restored. The National Park Authority has obviously decided that these are stables due to the occasional trough (most are replicas). They cannot be Solomon's, as they overlay one of his palaces that was destroyed by Shishak in 925 BCE. Rather, these stables date to the time of Omri and Ahab, and a number of archaeologists argue that the buildings were actually food storehouses.

A city in the ancient world needed several essential advantages: geographical height, a wall, stored grain and food, and water. The challenge was that the requirements of height and water supply were often at odds. This was because a spring, if present, would generally be at the base of the hill on which the city was built. Such was the case at Megiddo, which meant that the women had to walk outside the city wall each morning to gather water for the day, and

> **Tradition says that the final battle described in Revelation 16:16 will be fought here.**

thus the women and the water supply itself were vulnerable to enemy attack.

King Omri (or his son Ahab) solved this problem by building a 98-foot shaft and a 230-foot tunnel to the spring. Now water could be accessed safely from within the city walls. This will be your climactic exit from Tel Megiddo. As you descend the modern steps, look to your right to see the ancient steps. As you exit the tunnel, you can see the location of the spring to the left. Most tour groups will have their buses waiting for them at the water system exit.

Tiglath-pileser III conquered Megiddo in 732/33 BCE and made it the Assyrian capital of Galilee. Pharaoh Necho of Egypt slaughtered King Josiah of Judah here (2 Kings 23:29). So many cities; so many battles; so much destruction and renewal. It's little wonder that the book of Revelation (16:16) locates the apocalyptic Battle of battles here at Har Megiddo (Hebrew, the Hill of Megiddo; in Greek, *Armageddon).*

Tomb of Yehuda ha-Nasi

Galilee

Bet She'arim (National Park)

This is not only the most magnificent necropolis in the Holy Land but also a very good place to discuss the origin of rabbinic Judaism. When Jerusalem was destroyed by the Romans in 70 CE, the Sanhedrin relocated to Yavneh (Jamnia), just south of modern Tel Aviv. Then, at the conclusion of the Second Jewish Revolt (132–135 CE), the Sanhedrin moved to Galilee—first to Shfaram, then to Usha, then to Bet She'arim, and subsequently to Zippori (also known as *Sepphoris*), before finally settling in Tiberias.

Founded during the reign of King Herod the Great, Bet She'arim became part of the estate of his great-granddaughter Queen Berenice. Then, after the First Jewish Revolt, it became a possession of the Roman emperor. The leader of the Sanhedrin in the second century CE was the renowned rabbi Yehuda ha-Nasi (ca. 135–217 CE), who was evidently gifted the estate by his close friend since childhood, Emperor Marcus Aurelius (who was the Roman emperor from 161 to 180 CE).

Yehuda ha-Nasi is the redactor of the *Mishnah* (meaning "what is repeated"), the first written compilation of the oral law that was most closely associated with the Pharisaic sect of Judaism at the time of Jesus (see the discussion in the section on Caesarea). The Torah, the written law (Genesis–Deuteronomy), must be interpreted to be fulfilled. For example, "Remember the Sabbath day and treat it as holy" (Exodus 20:8) means what? What can be done or not done? How is the Sabbath sanctified as a day different from all the rest? The oral law that developed, especially from 200 BCE to 200 CE, answers these questions.

According to Jewish legend, when God gave Moses the written Instruction (the Torah), God whispered into Moses' ear the oral Instruction (its interpretation). Moses then repeated this to Joshua, Joshua repeated it to his successors, and so on until Ezra founded the Great Synagogue. From there came pairs of rabbis (Hillel and Shammai at the time of Jesus, for example) who faithfully passed on the tradition, so the legend goes. Thus it was extremely important for the rabbis that a teacher be part of this tradition; Jesus, however, came into conflict with this tradition since he claimed to be taught directly by God his Father.

The Mishnah was produced ca. 200 CE and became the authoritative scripture for an emerging rabbinical Judaism about the same time that the New Testament was being finalized as scripture for an emerging early Christianity. These were the only two sects of Judaism that remained of the many different kinds that existed at the time of Jesus. The Sadducees, Essenes, Zealots, and others perished with the two Jewish revolts. What we call Judaism and Christianity today are two religions of the same age, both tracing their roots to the Hebrew Bible (Old Testament), but with different centers to interpret these roots. For Judaism, the core is the Torah; for Christianity, the core is Jesus Christ. Rabbis continued to expound on the Mishnah with what became known as the Gemara (the Completion); and the Mishnah together with the Gemara form the Talmud (ca. 600 CE). The church fathers in about this same time frame likewise continued to interpret the New Testament with the authoritative Apostles', Nicene, and Athanasian Creeds.

Yehuda ha-Nasi moved the Sanhedrin to Bet She'arim, but when his health dictated a higher altitude, they moved to Zippori. Yet he returned to be buried in his beloved Bet She'arim where he had prepared his family tomb. At that time, Jews desired to be buried on the Mount of Olives, where they expected the Messiah to appear. But when that became impossible after 135 CE, when Hadrian turned Jerusalem into a Roman polis that was off-limits to Jews, what better place to await the resurrection of the dead than the burial place of the sainted Rabbi Yehuda ha-Nasi? Sadly, the prosperous town was destroyed in the mid-fourth century CE during a Jewish revolt against Byzantine rule and was rediscovered only in 1926 by Alexander Zaid, whose statue adorns the hill of the ancient city.

As you approach the necropolis, the ancient city is on your left with its synagogue and olive press. Upon arrival at the site, be sure to procure the national park brochure, which details a guided tour. In the center of the necropolis is the oldest burial cave with inscriptions all in Hebrew, many attributed to rabbis. Next door is the family tomb of Rabbi Yehuda

> **Jews expect the Messiah to appear on the Mount of Olives.**

ha-Nasi. Prior arrangement is necessary to assure entrance (phone: 04-983-1643; or ask for the key at the office adjacent to the parking lot). The rabbi insisted that he be buried in the ground, so we assume the subterranean graves in the far back and right are those of

> **From the earliest times, the Holy Land has been a mix of different cultures.**

himself and his wife (though there is no inscription). But we do have inscriptions to prove the graves of his two sons, Rabbi Gamaliel and Rabbi Shimon, as well as his student Rabbi Hanina. On the hill above each of these two central burial caves are meeting areas with benches for funerals, mourning, and remembering the dead.

The entire tour of the necropolis gives one an insight into Jewish life in the Galilee during the late second to mid-fourth centuries CE. Most inscriptions are in Hebrew, Aramaic, or Greek. Interestingly, the Greek inscriptions are associated with the more wealthy tombs, and Aramaic with the more common ones. Decorations include the traditional Jewish menorah, lulav (palm branch), ethrog (citron), incense shovel, shofar (horn), or ark of the covenant; as well as animals and figures from Greek mythology including Amazons, Aphrodite, Eros, and Nike. Entrance to the park must be at least one hour prior to closing time.

Zippori (National Park)

Also known as: Tsippori, Sepphoris

The Talmud says, "Why is it called Tsippori? Because it is perched on top of the mountain like a bird (tsippor)."[3] Josephus called Zippori "the ornament of all Galilee."[4] Herod took the city during his campaign to become "the Great,"[5] but upon his death the city rebelled and was destroyed by the Romans. It was totally rebuilt by Herod Antipas beginning in 3 BCE. Shortly before his death in 4 BCE, and true to his paranoid personality well attested by Josephus, Herod the Great sought to kill a baby rumored to be the Messiah—that is, a king who could usurp Herod's reign and that of his dynasty (Matthew 2). This led Jesus' earthly father, Joseph, to move his family to Egypt;

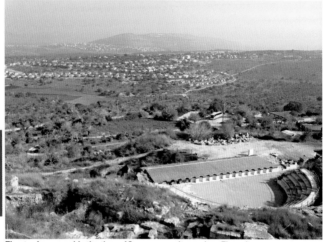

Theater from roughly the time of Jesus, opposite modern Zippori

but upon learning that Herod's son Archelaus was no better than the father, Joseph relocated to Nazareth, a small village of twelve to fifteen extended families at the time. This was likely so that he could exercise his profession as a builder[6] in the robustly growing city of Sepphoris only about three and a half miles away.

Immediately after the entrance kiosk, take a sharp left into the parking lot to view the waterworks. Since the time of Herod Antipas, aqueducts have supplied the city with mountain springwater from about three miles northeast. Follow the signs to the reservoir, which can be walked if the weather is dry. Then return to the parking lot and drive forward to the site's main entrance building. After a restroom break, gather in the gift shop theater to view the informative video. Then drive through the main-site entrance gate and follow the road to the right to the upper-city parking lot.

If time allows, descend the stairs from the parking lot to study the sixth/seventh-century CE synagogue. Then return to the parking lot and ascend the stairs to what is probably the oldest part of Zippori. At the top of several flights of stairs, make a sharp right and follow the path to the theater, which dates to the first or second century CE and seated about forty-five hundred people. On the principle of one seat for every ten residents, Herod Antipas's city grew steadily to a population of forty-five thousand. One can imagine that Jesus, who learned his earthly father's trade, had some acquaintance with the Roman theater, where he may

> Jesus may have worked in Sepphoris as a stonemason.

have learned the Greek word *hypokrites* (stage actor)—a term he would later apply in a critical way to certain Pharisees and scribes.[7]

Continue walking on the path up the tel, and you will soon come to a paved street with a cluster of dwellings dating from the first to the sixth centuries CE. The Jewish character of the town is obvious from the number of *mikvehs* (ritual baths), ritually clean stone vessels, and a lack of statues, a pagan temple, or pig bones, which would be absent due to Jewish dietary restrictions. It appears, however, to have been a rather liberal or progressive city, declining to take part in the First Jewish Revolt (66–70 CE) and taking a Greco-Roman name, Diocaesarea, after the Second Jewish Revolt (132–135 CE). The excavations of Tel Zippori, which began in 1931 and continue to the present day, reveal a city in which Jews, pagans, and Christians lived together in harmony.

Rabbi Judah ha-Nasi moved here from Bet She'arim for health reasons ca. 200 CE, with the Sanhedrin, or Jewish council, following him.[8] During the Byzantine period, the city became a bishopric. A short ascent to the summit of the tel will take you to the Crusader fortress, which underwent some renovation during the eighteenth and nineteenth centuries. From the top of the summit, look to the southeast to see the sprawling city of Nazareth along the top of the mountain. At the time of Jesus, Nazareth would have been a pastoral village and Zippori an emerging bustling metropolis.

The trail then leads to an impressive third-century CE villa, the center of which is the triclinium, or dining room, and around this are the living quarters. In the Roman period, fine mosaics of tiny stones were used much as we use Oriental carpets in our homes today. One can see where the dining tables were placed in a U-shape because the stones are simply solid white. The rest of the mosaic is a dramatic portrayal of the life of Dionysus, the god of wine. In the central panel he is engaged in a drinking contest with Hercules, who is inebriated and losing while Dionysus lifts his empty bowl-sized goblet upside down to show he is the winner. Another noteworthy panel is the beautiful woman (just in front of the viewing platform's lower level), evidently the matron of the house, whose winsome smile led archaeologists to dub her the "Mona Lisa of the Galilee."

You will now begin your descent of the tel to the lower city, following the path down the stairs through a cactus garden and by a Muslim cemetery—both of which are evidence that this was an Arab village of twelve thousand residents before the war of 1948. Pass the sifting apparatus on your right, showing that this is still an active dig, and the agora (market) on your left, to arrive at the center of the lower city. Here you will find the juncture of the *cardo* running north-south and the *decumanus*, a road running east-west—essential features of any Roman town. The *cardo* is what we today would call the mall. Note the wagon-wheel imprints in the limestone street, on either side of which was a colonnaded sidewalk with shops along the outside.

This public area leads past the "Orpheus House" to the so-called "Nile House," which may have been a public building. The central mosaic of the latter is a magnificent portrayal of the fertility of the Nile: A woman (Egypt) presides with cornucopia while the hippopotamus vomits out the Nile, which passes through fishermen, flora, and fauna to reach the lighthouse of Alexandria. Above, engineers measure the depth of the Nile, and below are various hunting scenes. Return by way of the *cardo*, turning right to the main entrance where you originally viewed the video. Meet your transportation there.

★ Nazareth

It is clear from the Gospels that the village of Nazareth was the home of Mary, Joseph, and their family during the years that Jesus grew from a boy into adulthood. Joseph's family was from Bethlehem, and Mary's was from Nazareth. Mary also had kin, Elizabeth and Zechariah, in the hill country near Bethlehem. We are not told where the engaged couple met; it could have been during one of Mary's visits to her kin in Judea, or Joseph could have visited Galilee seeking

Church of the Annunciation in Nazareth

Galilee

employment in Zippori. At any rate, in both Matthew and Luke, we find the couple engaged but not cohabiting (Matthew 1:18; Luke 1:27-34).[9] In Luke 2:1-7 we find Joseph accompanying Mary to his family home in Bethlehem, where she gave birth to Jesus. The family lived in Bethlehem for a time, probably with Joseph's parents, and then retreated to Egypt, the traditional place of refuge for Judeans (1 Kings 11:40; 2 Kings 25:26; Jeremiah 26:21).

To escape Herod's pogrom, they then moved to Nazareth, a poor village of only twelve to fifteen extended families, in order to be free of Herod's son and heir, Archelaus, in Judea. From there Joseph could get work in Herod Antipas's nearby booming new capital of the Galilee, Sepphoris (see the section on Zippori). The word used to describe Joseph's profession is *tekton* (Matthew 13:55; Mark 6:3), which means "artisan." A look around the Holy Land will quickly reveal that the building material is stone, not wood. Joseph was therefore a stonemason and an all-purpose builder. The anemic portrayals of our Lord are consequently misleading: the growing man who learned the trade of his earthly father was likely quite muscular.

Jesus is known in both the Gospels and Jewish sources as "the Nazarene" (Hebrew, *ha-Notsri*), and his early Jewish followers were called Nazarenes (Notsrim; see the section on Caesarea). The designation was a pregnant one because *Nazareth,* in Hebrew, *Natseret,* is a play on a common biblical term for the messiah, *netser,* or "branch." Nazareth is quite literally Branchtown! It is not surprising, then, that Julius Africanus (160–240 CE) mentions relatives

Galilee

> Perhaps Mary's home became a place where early Christians met to worship.

of Jesus in Nazareth. Between 249 and 251 CE, a man named Conon was martyred in Asia Minor after he testified, "I am from the city of Nazareth in Galilee. I am among the relatives of Christ to whom I have been offering homage since the days of my forefathers."[10] In 384 CE the early pilgrim Egeria was shown "a large cave" in which Mary had lived.

The current Basilica of the Annunciation, consecrated in 1969, follows the outline of the Crusader church. But before rebuilding, a thorough archaeological excavation revealed that the revered house of Mary is indeed part of the first-century village where the Holy Family lived. The excavation exposed an area replete with homes built next to caves used as barns (similar to the cave/barn of Jesus' birth in Bethlehem), grain silos, and other accessories of daily life.

When you enter the church, you are at the ground level. The north wall on your left was part of the Crusader church. Proceed to the far side of the area surrounded by a wrought-iron fence and, unless a Mass is in progress, you can descend the steps to the grotto, the revered house, obviously modified through the centuries. The pillars immediately to the left of the entrance to the grotto were added by the Crusaders, but the lower level on which you are standing is the Byzantine church. The apse (U-shaped section) of this earlier Byzantine church is clearly visible opposite the modern altar in the center of the octagonal space.

To the left of the grotto is a smaller cave, probably dedicated to Conon (mentioned above) at the time of his martyrdom. In front of this smaller cave are the remains of an early fourth-century CE church, including two mosaics in line with each other on a north-south axis, indicating that it is pre-Byzantine, perhaps from the time of Constantine.[11] The Greek inscription reads "Gift of Conon, deacon of Jerusalem," perhaps a relative of the martyr. Beneath this little church is a pre-Constantinian baptistery. The later, larger church (the U-shaped apse mentioned above) is built according to the Byzantine standard of an east-west axis. But beneath its floor was found a synagogue with Christian graffiti, including (in Greek) the first written occurrence anywhere of the short prayer "Hail Mary." This appears to have been the worship space of the Jewish Christian community stemming from the house church at the home of Mary.

We can conclude with some confidence that the venerated house beneath the modern church was the home of the Holy Family, and then of Mary at the time of Jesus' death and resurrection; and that, as happened at Peter's house in Capernaum, this became a house church of the Notsrim of Nazareth. The current modern church displays an inspirational collection of Madonnas donated from all over the world, and it is worth the time to peruse the courtyards around the church to see how various cultures portray the Virgin.[12]

The upper basilica is reached by ascending a spiral staircase at the end of the church where you originally entered. As you ascend from the dim light of veneration in the lower level to the celebratory brightness filling the upper level, you will see the magnificent mosaic in the front of the church depicting the one, holy, catholic (universal), and apostolic church. The center top portrays the Holy Trinity vertically with an eye in a triangle above a dove, above Jesus. To the left of Jesus is Mary, Mother of the Church and Queen of Heaven. To the right of Jesus is Peter (Matthew 16:13–20), and to the right of Peter are the apostles, from whom proceed the bishops of the church. On the left of the mosaic is the universal church, including the church triumphant.

Exit the upper basilica at the north wall, and beneath you are the excavations of first-century CE Nazareth. (The only restrooms are directly ahead up the stairs outside, and they cost two shekels to use.) Farther up the hill on the right is a church, built in 1914 on the outline foundations of a medieval church. It is certainly not the workshop of Joseph, a pious tradition from the seventeenth century CE without foundation. Beneath it there is evidence that first-century CE silos had been modified into a cavelike structure alongside a basin with seven steps, which could have been a baptistery of the early Christian community of Nazareth.

To visit the archaeological excavation and the museum with the artifacts found therein, call the museum curator Edwardo ahead of time for a reservation (phone: 050-937-7689). He gives a good tour for five shekels per person, and it is recommended to add a tip. Alternatively, you can call the office (phone: 04-657-2501). The basilica is open daily from 8:30 a.m. to 5:00 p.m. (to 6 p.m. in summer), but the excavation and museum are closed from noon to 2 p.m. for lunch. And since this is an active Palestinian congregation, the church is open on Sunday mornings only if you are attending Mass.

The Greek Orthodox Church of the Annunciation is located on the northern edge of town, rather than near where the Roman Catholic tradition locates Mary's home. This is probably due to a passage in the apocryphal Protogospel of James 10,1–11,3 that narrates the appearance of the angel Gabriel to Mary near a spring. The apocryphal Gospel of Thomas also mentions the boy Jesus carrying water from a spring. The location known today as Mary's Well, or the Church of St. Gabriel, traces its roots to a shrine built on the spring in 326 CE. Destroyed and rebuilt several times, the current church dates to the seventeenth century CE and was expanded in the eighteenth century.

The well cannot claim much authenticity. A better use of your time would be a visit to Nazareth Village, a modern re-creation of Jewish life in Nazareth at the time of Jesus, and an excellent follow-up to the excavations and museum discussed above. This tour is guided, and reservations are necessary for groups. Open Monday–Saturday, 9 a.m.–5 p.m. (Phone: 04-645-6042; website: www.nazarethvillage.com.)

Tiberias

Herod Antipas (4 BCE–39 CE) followed in the footsteps of his dad, who built Caesarea on the Mediterranean coast, by founding his own coastal city on the shores of the Sea of Galilee and naming it after Tiberius Caesar (14–37 CE). It was constructed in 17–20 CE upon a cemetery, which is why Antipas had to force Jews to move here. Ironically, it eventually became the center of Jewish learning after the destruction of the Temple in 70 CE.

Rabbi Johanan ben Nappaha (180–297 CE), a disciple of Rabbi Judah ha-Nasi (ca. 135–217 CE; see the sections on Bet She'arim and Zippori), is responsible for the establishment of Tiberias's rabbinical school in the year 235 CE. Judah ha-Nasi had compiled the Oral Law

Tiberias overloooks the Sea of Galilee

Galilee

(the rabbinical interpretation of the Written Torah) into what became known as the Mishnah, completed around 200 CE. The rabbis of Tiberias then composed commentary upon the Mishnah that became known as the Gemara, completed around 400 CE. The Palestinian Talmud comprises this Mishnah and Gemara.

Furthermore, students of Hebrew will know that the Torah itself is written without vowels. To preserve the traditional correct reading of the words, the rabbinic family of Ben Asher worked in Tiberias during the eighth to the tenth centuries CE to produce a system of "vowel points"—dots and dashes surrounding the letters of the Torah that do not disturb the sacred consonants, which are still used in seminaries today. So it is not surprising that many of rabbinic Judaism's most influential sages are buried in the city center of Tiberias: Rabbi Yohanan ben Zakkai (first century CE); Rabbi Eliezer ben Hyrcanus (second century CE); Rabbi Moses ben Maimon (twelfth century CE); and up on the hillside beneath the white dome, Rabbi Akiva, who was a leader in the academy of Yavneh (Jamnia). This academy was responsible for what became the canon of the Hebrew Bible (Old Testament). Rabbi Akiva unfortunately acclaimed Bar Kochva the Messiah during the Second Jewish Revolt (132–135 CE), for which the Romans executed him.

The nascent excavations of ancient Tiberias have not been well preserved, and so they are recommended only for those with extra time on their hands. They can be reached from a parking lot on the main coastal road (Highway 90), across from the Sironit

Beach between downtown and Khame-Teveria (Tiberias Hot Springs), at the southern edge of town.

> Tiberias was a popular hot springs resort for wealthy Romans, one that you can also enjoy.

Indeed worth a visit is Hamat Tverya (National Park and museum), located across the street from the modern Tiberias Hot Springs spa (also very much worth a place on your agenda). The popular hot springs resort probably accounts for why Antipas chose this site for his city. At the center of the excavation is a fourth-century CE synagogue that gives a glimpse into Jewish life in Tiberias at that time. The top panel of the magnificent mosaic floor depicts the traditional Jewish symbol of the ark surrounded by menorahs, lulavs (palm branches), ethrogs (citrons), shofars (horns), and incense shovels, all reminiscent of the Temple. But in the center is the sun god Helios, surrounded by a zodiac in which the months are properly aligned with the seasons, and the names are in Hebrew. In the bottom panel between two lions are eight inscriptions in Greek devoted to donors, especially Severus, who had close ties with the rabbinic academy of Tiberias discussed above. The mosaic also includes one inscription in Aramaic.

The museum is dedicated to the history of the hot springs, but note that it is closed on Shabbat. For a swim in the spa across the street, bring your bathing suit; a towel is provided. There is an inside pool, but best is the outside pool alongside the Sea of Galilee. The view is spectacular, and the warm waters make the experience possible even on winter evenings. There is also an outside cold water pool. The spa is open until 10 p.m. on Tuesdays and Thursdays, but closes at 4 p.m. on Fridays. Open until 5 p.m. on Shabbat and until 8 p.m. the other nights.

An economical yet very nice place to stay while touring Tiberias and the Galilee is the Royal Plaza Hotel, just across the street from the modern hot springs on the coast of the Sea of Galilee (phone: 04-670-0000; website: www.royalplaza.co.il/index.php/english).

Galilean hills around the sea

★ Sea of Galilee

Also known as: Sea of Kinneret, Chinnereth Sea

The Hebrew name is *Yam Kinneret* (Sea of Kinneret; Numbers 34:11; Joshua 12:3; 13:27), from the word *kinnor*, a handheld harp or lyre. It is roughly shaped like David's harp, wider at the top than at the bottom; and many have been soothed by the music of its gentle waves lapping along the shore. At about seven hundred feet below sea level, it is the lowest freshwater lake on the planet. In Greek, as in English, the word *sea* denotes a body of salt water; so the locals in the first century called it the Lake of Gennesaret (Luke 5:1; Josephus). "The Sea of Galilee" is a unique early Christian toponym based on the belief that Jesus is the fulfillment of Isaiah's ancient prophecy (Isaiah 9:1).

> He went to Galilee. He left Nazareth and settled in Capernaum, which lies alongside the sea in the area of Zebulun and Naphtali. This fulfilled what Isaiah the prophet said: *Land of Zebulun and land of Naphtali, alongside the sea, across the Jordan, Galilee of the Gentiles, the people who lived in the dark have seen a great light, and a light has come upon those who lived in the region and in shadow of death.* (Matthew 4:12b-16)

In the Isaiah passage, "the way of the sea" (Isaiah 9:1) is the highway from upper Galilee to Tyre on the Mediterranean coast, but the congruence of "alongside the sea, across the Jordan, Galilee of the Gentiles" prompted early Christians to identify the passage with the region of Jesus' ministry, and so the lake became "the Sea of Galilee" in their nomenclature. Matthew, Mark, and John employ the term; Luke prefers the more historical-geographical term *lake* (Luke 8:22). The theologically pregnant toponym "the Sea of Galilee" also recalls Jesus walking on the sea and stilling the storm on the sea, which echo God's mastery of the Sea at creation (Genesis 1; Psalms 74:12-17; 89:9; 104:2-9).

The Sea of Galilee is formed by the Jordan River on its northern shore and is approximately thirteen miles long, seven and a half miles wide, and 140 feet deep. It is surrounded by mountains and wadis (valleys), which account for the rise of sudden storms, especially in the winter, when the winds rush down to stir up its otherwise tranquil waters. It supplies the Holy Land with fresh water for drinking and irrigation, and it supports a vibrant fishing industry, now as in the time of Jesus.

You will want to take a boat ride, and there are a number of licensed companies; a good one is Kinneret Sailing (website: www.eingev.co.il/?CategoryID=289). When reserving your boat, you can also reserve your lunch at the Ein Gedi Kibbutz fish restaurant, whose specialty is "St. Peter's Fish," indigenous to the Sea of Galilee. Sailing routes are to and from En Gev, Tiberias, Ginosar, and Capernaum; so plan your boat ride route accordingly so it works best with your itinerary.

Arbel (National Park) and Magdala

Whether you are driving along the highway or observing from your boat ride, just north of Tiberias is a juncture marked by a steep cliff (Arbel) and a valley (Wadi Arbel or Wadi Hammam; sometimes called the Valley of the Doves). The natural path through the valley leads west to Cana and then south to Zippori and Nazareth. This was the path Jesus took when he traveled from his hometown of Nazareth to his adopted home around the sea, Capernaum. The path meets the Sea of Galilee beneath Mount Arbel at Magdala, home of Mary Magdalene. Excavation is taking place on the coastal side of the

Mount Arbel astride the Valley of the Doves

highway, just south of its modern namesake, Migdal. The original Hebrew name, *Migdal-Nunia* (fish tower; Greek, *Taricheae*, salted fish), referred to the village's major industry, the drying of fish caught in the abundant Sea of Galilee.

Galilee

Archaeologists debate whether the building you see in the ruins is a synagogue or a spring tower. The most famous find here was a first-century mosaic depicting an exact replica of the first-century fishing boat discovered by, and on display at, Kibbutz Ginosar. (A slide of the mosaic is displayed behind the boat in the Yigal Allon Center.) New excavations in Magdala have extended to the north where, in 2009, archaeologists unearthed a first-century CE synagogue, in the center of which is a rectangular stone with an impressive menorah (the first to be found dating to a synagogue from the period when the Temple was still standing). Guided visits can be arranged Monday–Sunday, 8 a.m.–6 p.m., but the guide must be reserved in advance (phone: +972-4-620-9900; e-mail: visit@magdala.org; website: www.magdala.org).

The most striking feature of Arbel is the one hundred caves within its slope, which were the scene of bloody battles during the Maccabean (161 BCE)[13] and Herodian (38 BCE)[14] wars, as well as the First Jewish Revolt (66–70 CE).[15] The view from the top is spectacular, and the caves are reachable from there (or from the road below).

> **See the spectacular view and witness the scene of many ancient battles.**

Ginosar

Also known as: Gennesar, Gennesaret

Just north of Mount Arbel and Magdala is the fertile plain of Ginosar. Rabbinic sages[16] trace the etymology to the Hebrew *gane hasarim* (*gan*, garden; *sar*, prince; "the gardens of the princes"), evidently a reference to the Hasmoneans. Josephus[17] describes the fecund soil and perfect weather as producing virtually every species of tree. Today, Kibbutz Nof (view of) Ginosar sits serenely on the shore and provides not only an essential stop for the student-pilgrim, but also an excellent place to lodge during your stay at the Sea of Galilee.

In 1986, during a severe drought when the level of the lake was very low, two brothers from the kibbutz discovered a fishing boat buried in the seabed. Affectionately called "the Jesus boat" by the locals, it dates to the first centuries before and after Jesus' time. It is congruent with the boats referred to in the Gospels, in accounts of battles during the First Jewish Revolt (67–70 CE), and as portrayed in the Magdala mosaic, which is pictured in the museum. Twelve different types of wood were used in its construction and repairs, so the members of the kibbutz have lovingly planted those twelve

First-century CE boat with Magdala mosaic

species of trees to line the entrance to the museum where the boat is housed. The boat, whose approximate dimensions are twenty-seven feet long, seven and a half feet wide, and four feet high, could hold four men.

Enter the Yigal Allon Center from the parking lot. Restrooms are to the right, and the ticket counter is in the middle. After paying for your ticket, you may pass through the automatic doors at the far end of the building, and a short video will begin explaining how the boat was found and preserved. If you prefer, you can request at the ticket counter to see the longer, full-length version of this film. In addition, the Center boasts four floors of exhibitions on the history, culture, and ecology of the Galilee. Open Sunday–Thursday, 8 a.m.–5 p.m.; Friday and holiday eves, 8 a.m.–2 p.m.; Shabbat and holidays, 8 a.m.–4 p.m.

The Nof Ginosar Kibbutz Hotel (website: www.english.ginosar. co.il) is a favorite place to stay on the Sea of Galilee. Though most of the rooms do not have a direct view of the sea because of the lush vegetation, there are walking trails to the beach and spectacular sunsets behind Mount Arbel. The lobby is recently renovated, the rooms are stylishly simple, and perhaps most significantly, the food is among the best of any place in the Holy Land.

Tabgha and Mount of Beatitudes

Though Tabgha and the Mount of Beatitudes are traditional and not historical sites, they are worth a visit to recall the Gospel narratives associated with them. Tabgha is an Arabic corruption of the Greek *Heptapegon* (seven springs), which is associated with the multiplication of the loaves and fishes (Mark 6:30-44) and the primacy of Peter (John 21).

The Church of the Multiplication in Tabgha is a replica, built in 1982, of the fifth-century CE church, but much of the mosaic floor is original. Glass panes in the floor reveal remains of the original and smaller fourth-century CE church. Beneath the altar is a rock, venerated at least since the fifth century CE as the table upon which our Lord performed the miracle. The fourth-century CE pilgrim Egeria mentions such a rock, but she also says it is beside some stone steps, which better matches the rock within the chapel of the primacy of Peter. It is possible that the pre-Byzantine tradition associated the rock at the primacy of Peter with the feeding of the five thousand, but in the Byzantine period, that tradition shifted to the rock in the Church of the Multiplication. The original rock then became associated with the breakfast on the beach of John 21.

Church of the Multiplication

At any rate, the mosaic beneath the altar in the Church of the Multiplication is the most famous in the country. Within the basket are four round pita loaves (Hebrew, *kikrot lekhem*). The feeding of the five thousand is the only narrative included in all four Gospels (except the Passion Narrative, which was the earliest narrative to congeal as central to the faith of the early church). Clearly for the early church, the narrative of the multiplication was second in importance only to the narrative of Jesus' death and resurrection. Why? To get at this answer, we must ask, "Where is the fifth loaf?" Obviously, it is on the altar. The narrative of the multiplication is not only about something that happened, but about what happens in every Eucharist, hence Jesus' words to his disciples: "You give them something to eat" (Mark 6:37; cf. John 6:26-58).

On either side of the loaves and fishes mosaic are two of the most stunning and detailed mosaics in the Holy Land. They depict flora, fauna, and daily life around the Sea of Galilee, and as such provide a delightful and realistic setting

> The mosaic beneath the altar in the Church of the Multiplication is the most famous in the country.

for the central panel beneath the altar. The lotus flower motif comes from the Nile, not the Galilee. It is reminiscent of the Nile mosaic at Zippori, as is the pillar with engineers measuring the depth of the lake. Note that the church is closed on Sundays.

The Church of the Primacy of Peter is a chapel built in 1933 on the ruins of a fourth-century CE church, alongside steps that can be seen outside on the beach side, enshrining a table rock. As noted above, the setting matches Egeria's description, and regardless of what this rock table commemorated in her day (her description is not completely transparent), it became associated with the two stories in John 21: the postresurrection appearance of Jesus through breakfast on the beach, and Jesus' threefold injunction to Peter to feed his sheep. This is the best place to spend twenty minutes in solitude at the shore of the sea. As you descend beside the ancient steps, note the six heart-shaped stones that supported six pairs of pillars associated with the apostles.

Across the street are the remains of the fourth-century CE Church of the Sermon of the Mount, the mosaics of which are displayed at Capernaum. It was replaced in 1938 with the chapel designed by the Italian architect Antonio Barluzzi on the summit of what has become known as the Mount of Beatitudes, built as an octagon inscribing the eight beatitudes in Latin (Matthew 5:3-10). Holy Communion may be celebrated at one of the many altars (inside or outside) by prior reservation with the sisters of the convent. The view is spectacular, and at the very least time should be allotted here for meditation.

★ Capernaum

We discussed under the section on Arbel and Magdala how Jesus traveled from his hometown of Nazareth to his home base at the Sea of Galilee, Capernaum (Hebrew, *Kefar Nakhum*; the village of Nahum). Indeed, during the period of his Galilean ministry he evidently dwelt here so often that Matthew can call it "his own city" (9:1). The centerpiece of

> Peter's family home became an early house church.

View of Peter's house from the synagogue

the excavations here is Peter's family house (Mark 1:29-31), where Jesus lived, since Mark can say of it, "After a few days, Jesus went back to Capernaum, and people heard that he was at home" (2:1).

At Tabgha we dealt with traditional sites, but here we are on firm historical ground. The evidence: The archaeological remains inside Peter's house include the normal accoutrements of daily life in a family home before about 50 CE. After that time, we find only lamps and large jars, items one would expect in a public meeting hall. The room was plastered to set it apart from any other rooms in the area, and in the plaster we found graffiti mentioning Jesus as Messiah and Lord. Clearly there was a change in the usage of this house sometime in the mid-first century CE from a private dwelling to a public building, and the most reasonable explanation is that Peter's family home, which he shared with his brother Andrew, his mother-in-law, and Jesus (Mark 1:29-31; 2:1), became an early *domus ecclesia*, or house church.

It would have had a roof of mud and branches, which is the one "some people . . . tore off" in Mark 2:3-4 so that Jesus could heal the paralytic. In the fourth century CE, the room was given a stronger roof with a supporting arch, and extra rooms were added around it. It is this church that the pilgrim Egeria saw in 381–384 CE when she wrote, "Moreover, in Capernaum the house of the prince of the apostles has been made into a church, with its original walls still standing. It is where the Lord healed the paralytic."

In the fifth century CE, the additional rooms were razed to make way for an octagonal church built around the venerated room, which received a mosaic floor depicting a peacock surrounded by lotus flowers, similar to the Church of the Multiplication (see the section on Tabgha). The modern church with its glass floor sits atop the original and replicates its octagonal shape. Just in front of the church, the statue of Peter holding a large key (see Matthew 16:19) commemorates the visit of Pope John Paul II to Capernaum.

The black stone building material of Peter's house (first century CE) is basalt, a reminder of upper Galilee's volcanic past. Capernaum at the time of Jesus was a modest village of one- or two-room one-story houses grouped around common courtyards, which provided outdoor space for ovens, grinding stones, and daily work. A good example of this is the excavation (Insula II) between Peter's house and the synagogue.

Towering over the basalt ruins is the partially reconstructed fourth-century CE limestone synagogue, the most famous and largest one excavated in the Holy Land. Its three entrance doors face south to Jerusalem, and on its eastern side is a courtyard (roofed on three sides), replete with children's games etched into the pavement. This is the synagogue that Egeria saw and wrote about in her diary: "There is also the synagogue where the Lord cured a man possessed by the devil [Mark 1:21-28]. The way in is up many stairs, and it is made of dressed stone." Its foundation is the black basalt first-century CE synagogue in which Jesus preached (Luke 4:31; John 6:59).

New Testament Capernaum was poor enough that the people needed a Roman centurion to build it for them (Luke 7:5). He was probably a God-fearer (that is, a Gentile who went to synagogue and believed in God but had not actually converted to Judaism; see the section on Caesarea). But the fact that he was stationed here indicates that the humble town was important enough to house a Roman garrison as well as a tax/customs office (Matthew 9:9). This was because it was the entry point for travelers coming from Bethsaida and the largely Gentile territory of Herod Philip (the "other side" of the Jordan River) to the largely Jewish territory of Herod Antipas,

Tetrarch of Galilee (see Mark 4:35; 5:1). The basalt steps just outside the northern wall of the limestone synagogue (exit north from the courtyard and turn left) may have led to an upper floor in the first-century CE structure that may in turn have served as a gallery for women. However, it is not certain that the genders were separated during worship at the time of Jesus.

Bethsaida

This site on the Sea of Galilee's northern shore has only recently been certified to be biblical Bethsaida because it is currently so far inland. But the earthquake of 363 CE dammed up the Jordan River for a period of time until it burst forth to release its retained sediment and extend its bank beyond Bethsaida, well over a mile into the Sea of Galilee. At that time the fishing town evidently moved to el-Araj, now closer to the shore, which is the other tel that had previously been associated with Bethsaida.

Fisherman's house

The community that became known as Bethsaida (House of the Fisherman) was settled during the Hellenistic period and made a Jewish village by Herod the Great. It was the home of some of Jesus' first disciples: Philip, Peter and his brother Andrew, and perhaps their business partners, the Zebedee brothers James and John (Luke 5:7-11). With Capernaum and Korazim, Bethsaida completes the so-called "Gospel Triangle" of cities where Jesus spent most of his Galilean ministry.

The entrance fee to the excavations of Bethsaida is not included on the national park ticket and must be paid in cash at the parking lot, where clean restrooms are available. The walking path is clearly marked with an introductory sign. Follow it, and

> **Bethsaida was the home of Peter, Andrew, and Philip, but also perhaps of James and John.**

you will find yourself on the first-century CE street.

On the left are two large houses that were evidently in use for a long period of time. The first has been termed the "House of the Winegrower," because of its basalt-stone wine cellar, indicating a wealthy owner since wine cellars were generally used for a collection of imported wines. Note in the kitchen area the grinding stones (the upper one was unfortunately stolen) that would have taken two women to work (Matthew 24:41). Just down the street is the "House of the Fisherman," so named for the many accessories of the fisherman's trade found therein: anchors, lead and net weights, fishhooks, and needles for mending nets and sails, as well as a large key. The key led some of the archaeologists to nickname the house "Peter's House," after Matthew 16:19. Walk to the end of the path for a scenic overlook of many of the biblical sites related to Jesus' ministry.[18]

Bethsaida was the first town one would have reached in traveling west to east, crossing the Jordan River where it flows into the Sea of Galilee from the north. By so doing, one left the territory of Herod Antipas (Galilee) and entered the territory of Herod Philip, "the other side" as the Gospels call it when speaking from the more Jewish/Galilean perspective (Mark 5:1).[19] In 30 CE Herod Philip renamed Bethsaida "Julias" after the recently deceased wife of Caesar Augustus, Livia/Julia. Excavators have identified a temple dedicated to her that contains accoutrements of her cult, including her figurine, incense shovels, and a coin minted by Herod Philip, which depicts her holding ears of grain relating to her role as a fertility goddess, with the inscription in Greek "*carpophoros*" (bearer of fruit). Perhaps Jesus chose to use these same words to explain that his mission must include his Passion, because he knew that this phrase was one they could understand: "unless a grain of wheat falls into the earth and dies, it can only be a single seed. But if it dies, it *bears* much *fruit*" (John 12:24; emphasis added).[20]

Turn around to return, and make a sharp right on a small trail that leads down to the Old Testament site that was the capital of Geshur, perhaps named Zer. King David's third wife, Maachah, was from here; so their son Absalom also stayed here in the city of his maternal grandfather (2 Samuel 3:3). As you descend, you will note a huge Iron Age gate, the largest in Israel, with *matsevot* (standing stones) at each of its four corners, marking it off as holy space. It has four chambers, and if you look closely, you can see that when the Assyrian king Tiglath-pileser III destroyed the city in 732 BCE (2 Kings 15:29), the fires burned so fiercely that the mud bricks actually melted.

Continue forward to exit the gate. Turn left to see at the gate's outer right-hand corner a stepped high place with a cultic basin and stela showing a god with a bull's head whose crescent-shaped horns may indicate it was the moon god. Continue left along the ancient street outside the city wall, along the path that leads back to the parking lot.

Korazim (National Park)

Also known as Chorazin

View from Korazim to Bethsaida

> **Some synagogues contain art depicting Greek mythology.**

Almost nine hundred feet above the Sea of Galilee, Korazim completes, with Capernaum and Bethsaida, the "Gospel Triangle" where Jesus spent most of his Galilean ministry. Korazim grew when Jews from Judea moved to Galilee after being expelled by Hadrian in 135 CE due to the Second Jewish Revolt. But the Onomasticon (collection of writings) of Eusebius (ca. 263–339 CE) describes Korazim as lying in ruin. The town was restored in the late fourth century CE and lasted into the eighth century, spreading over eighty to one hundred acres. Jewish life returned to the village in the Middle Ages.

At the entrance, the restrooms are on the right. Continue forward on the path past the entrance kiosk, and on your right is the town mikveh and two adjacent cisterns, all roofed. To better view these structures, exit the path to the right. Return to the main path and continue into a housing area for extended families built around a central square. The arrows will lead you farther to the fourth-century CE synagogue that is similar to the one at Capernaum, except that this one is built of black basalt, the building stone of upper Galilee and a remnant of its volcanic past. The entrance faces Jerusalem, and inside on the left is the ark housing the Torah scroll. On the right is the Seat of Moses for the Torah reader/leader of the synagogue (Matthew 23:2). The synagogue is richly decorated. Some of the decorations include a conch, typical of Byzantine synagogues, and even a Medusa. (Use of art from Greek mythology was also not unusual during this period.) If time allows, exit the synagogue down the stairs and turn right to the twelfth–thirteenth century CE buildings with their olive oil presses.

Tel Hazor (National Park)

Also known as: Khatzor

The raison d'être for the location of this ancient metropolis is the same as that for Megiddo and Bet She'an: it is at a crossroads, in this case between Syria and Mesopotamia to the east, the Mediterranean to the west, and Canaan/Israel to the south. It boasted thirty thousand inhabitants spread over two hundred acres in the Canaanite period. It was clearly, as the book of Joshua says, "the head of all those kingdoms" (11:10), referring to the many city-states of Canaan. This is why King Jabin and his general Sisera (Joshua 11; Judges 4–5) gathered the Canaanite city-states in battle against the emerging proto-Israelites settling in the hill country and evidently spreading into the Galilee. These "Israelites" defeated the forces of the coalition and, according to Joshua 11:1-12, destroyed Hazor. The archaeological excavation confirms a violent destruction of the city by fire in about 1200 BCE; the location of an olive oil storage facility near the palace accounts for the more than three feet of ashes found there by the excavators.

Recent excavations at Gezer and Khirbet Qeiyafa confirm the account in 1 Kings of Solomon's building projects: "This is the story of the labor gang that King Solomon put together to build the LORD's temple and his own palace, as well as the stepped structure, the wall of Jerusalem, Hazor, Megiddo, and Gezer" (9:15). The three-chambered gates at the latter three cities are almost identical, and it is at this gate that your walking tour begins. Beneath are the ruins of a Canaanite temple, and

Canaanite shrine beneath Iraelite fortress

as you walk through the gate, you can see to your left the adjoining casemate wall that extended all the way up toward the citadel on the northwestern ridge (now adorned by the figure of an Israelite soldier).

Proceed forward to the Canaanite palace, now under a large protective roof. Pass the monumental platform and bear right up the ancient stairs between two huge pillars to enter the throne room, which originally had a wooden floor, surrounded by rooms on three sides. The basalt slabs support mud-brick walls (the restored bricks were made from the remains of the original ones), interspersed with cedar-beam anchors for paneling (cf. King David's "cedar palace" [2 Samuel 7:2]).

Exit the palace the same way you entered, but as you pass the monumental platform, turn right up the hill and follow the path to the waterworks. In the ninth century BCE, the population of the city doubled. King Ahab expanded the city walls and, in light of the emerging Assyrian threat, secured a water supply within the city by having his engineers reach the aquifer 130 feet below the surface. As you descend the modern metal staircase, note the original eighty stairs cut into the rock by which the women would have descended each morning to get the household's water supply for the day.

Immediately above the waterworks and to the right side of the walking path are two Israelite buildings. These originally stood above the Canaanite palace but were moved to their present location so they could be better viewed, and also so the palace could be excavated. The first is the "four-room house" typical of the Israelite period. You can enter the open-air working courtyard, this one with its own olive oil press. The meat of the olives, which had been crushed away from the pits with a heavy rolling stone, was placed in burlap bags such as you see in this restoration. They were then further crushed by the weight of hanging stones to release more oil that flowed into an adjoining receptacle. To your right is the barn, and straight ahead and to your left are living quarters. The living quarters all have a roof of wood, (palm) branches, and mud. The building just beyond the house was a storage facility, which also would have been roofed and would have held preserved food to provide for the Israelite city under attack.

Exit the Israelite house, turn right, and head all the way up the hill to the Israelite citadel. From the platform overlook, peer down to view a circular Canaanite shrine from the period of the judges (twelfth–eleventh centuries BCE). Note the large erect phallus (*matsevah*), a symbol of male fertility. The terebinth tree, which often grows in a vulval shape, may also have been part of the cultic area. One is reminded of the later Deuteronomic prohibition of shrines, standing stones (*matsevot*), and sacred trees.

Return to your transportation. As you exit the Tel Hazor National Park, turn left onto Highway 90 toward Kiryat Shmona (to the north). Immediately at the first junction to the right (the road to Kibbutz Ayelet Hashahar) is the Hazor Museum, which displays most of the original artifacts found at Tel Hazor. It is well worth a visit.

Galilee

Tel Dan (National Park)

Tel Dan National Park provides a multidimensional experience, including a nature hike through what the Israelis call their "Garden of Eden," archaeological excavations of the biblical period, and a glimpse into modern political realities, so allow two to three hours. The tribe of Dan had originally settled on the Mediterranean

Jeroboam's altar and temple at Dan

A tablet with an inscription claiming victory over "the House of David" is in the Israel Museum in Jerusalem.

coast south of Jaffa. But the Philistines pushed them out, so they traveled north to this location (originally a Canaanite city called Laish) to expel the Canaanites and rename the city after their eponym. Jeroboam I, after leading the ten northern tribes that seceded from the kingdom of David and Solomon, made Dan his northern border and erected a golden calf on a shrine here, parallel to the one at Bethel on his southern border. Omri and Ahab rebuilt the city in the ninth century BCE, and it was evidently destroyed by Tiglath-pileser III during his invasion of 732 BCE.

As you enter the park, be sure to receive the descriptive brochure outlining the various hiking trails. Proceed to the parking lot, where restrooms are available. The tour begins with a hike through the nature reserve alongside the Dan spring, which, along with the Senir (Hatzbani) and Hermon (Banias) streams, forms the Jordan River. The entrance to the trail is to the right of the gift shop. If you are part of a group with a bus driver, have him meet you at the exit outside the Israelite gate. If you are on your own, you will need to plan a hike that brings you back to the parking lot. The first part of the trail is wheelchair-accessible to all. At the juncture of the long trail and the short trail, only the physically fit should continue. The long trail is recommended, bearing right at the juncture toward the "Garden of Eden" and emerging alongside the Israelite city walls, buttressed for strength, and gates.

Enter the outer gate, walking on the smooth pavement, and turn left through the middle gate where the pivots for the doors are visible. As at Bethsaida, a shrine with *matzevot* stands at the entrance.[21] Straight ahead is a bench where the elders sat, and to its left is a podium supporting a canopy where the king would sit for "judgment at the gate" (2 Samuel 15:2). To the left of the throne, pass through the double-chambered gate, noting the door pivots and doorstop. Continue up the paved street to a fourth gate that was added in the eighth century BCE (on the left is another shrine/altar). Proceed on the modern path to the main cultic shrine, originally erected by Jeroboam I. The outlines of the altar have been reproduced for you with a stainless steel frame. Behind this is the foundation for the temple housing the golden calf, upon which the God of Israel was understood to be present, on the analogy of the Canaanite Ba'al, who is regularly represented as standing on a calf or a bull. Hence Jeroboam, lacking the ark of the covenant, the traditional Israelite throne of God, borrowed from Canaanite culture, thereby endearing himself to his subjects with the proclamation, "Look, Israel! Here are your gods who brought you out from the land of Egypt" (1 Kings 12:28).

Continue ascending the slope to the right (if you are facing the altar), walking either on the external path or through the Israeli bunker for a view of the Lebanese border. Keep on going forward and turn left at the T on the trail, which will lead you past the Canaanite middle Bronze Age gate (mid-eighteenth century BCE), through which Abraham and Sarah conceivably could have passed. The triple arches, now supported with wooden beams, were well preserved when originally excavated, as can be observed on the drawing at the site. Continue forward on the path, past restrooms, to the exit gate to meet your transportation.

On your way to the Kiryat Shmona–Banias Road, stop if time allows at the Bet Ussishkin regional nature and archaeological museum, presenting flora and fauna of the Golan as well as artifacts from the tel's excavation. Note, however, that the most famous find from Tel Dan is in the Israel Museum (Jerusalem): the tablet from the second half of the ninth century BCE with an inscription of Hazael, king of Damascus, claiming victory over the king of Israel and the king of the House of David (*bet david*)—the first time the inscription "the House of David" has been found outside the Bible.

Caesarea Philippi (National Park)

Also known as: Hermon Stream (Banias) Nature Reserve

Alexander the Great conquered the Middle East in 332 BCE, bringing with him his Greek culture. When he died prematurely, his general Seleucus became the ruler of Syria, and another general, Ptolemy, became the ruler of Egypt. Israel, lying between them, was under the sway of the Ptolemies until the battle here at Paneas (or

Galilee

"Gates of Hell"

Banias) in 200 BCE, when the Seleucids became Israel's overlord. The place is so named because of the Panaeon, or temple to the nature god Pan, constructed here and mentioned by the historian Xenon of Rhodes, who reports the above-mentioned battle. Some of the shrines east of the cave are dated by their Greek inscriptions to the second century CE; so the cult of Pan continued here for quite some time.

Caesar Augustus gave the surrounding territory to Herod the Great, who in gratitude built a temple dedicated to Augustus just opposite the cave. His son Herod Philip inherited this area that we now call the Golan Heights and made Paneas his capital, renaming it Caesarea Philippi. It remained the capital under Agrippa II, who further enhanced and expanded the city. A Jewish community remained here throughout the second and third centuries CE. With the rise of the Byzantine (Christian) empire in the fourth century CE, the Paneaon was abandoned, but Caesarea Philippi/Paneas continued to be a vibrant city until the Muslim conquest in the seventh century CE. The city of Banias, as it became known in Arabic (which lacks the letter *p*), arose once again during the tenth through the twelfth centuries CE with Muslim, Jewish, and Christian presences. However, it was a small Syrian village when Israel acquired the Golan Heights in the 1967 Six-Day War.

If you approach the national park from Kiryat Shmona, as most do, you will see that Highway 99 divides the modern excavations, with the older Panaeon to the left and King Agrippa II's expansion with palace and Crusader city walls to the right. Turn to the left into the parking lot through the ticket booth. Be sure to keep your receipt in case you wish to visit Banias Falls later. Restrooms are hidden far left of the parking lot, accessible either by walking through the wooded picnic area or by walking up past the gift shop and left along the Banias pools, then left again.

Looking up from the parking lot you can't miss the huge cave, which explains why the Panaeon was located here. Originally the cave was the source of the spring, which now emerges below due to seismic shifts. It was so deep that it was evidently thought to be the gates of Hades, connected to the Underworld and the river Styx itself. What better place than this, which had been associated with the fertility god Ba'al Hermon during the Old Testament period, to locate the cult of Pan, god of fertility, and to offer sacrifices to the gods by hurling them into the cave? As you stand in front of the cave today, immediately to your left are the remains of Herod's temple dedicated to Caesar Augustus, and to your right are temples and shrines of the Panaeon, with niches for idols of Pan, his consort Echo, and his father, Hermes.

You might also reflect on what happened in the life of Jesus while standing here. The Gospels report that after Herod Antipas of Galilee murdered John the Baptist, Jesus took his disciples outside the jurisdiction of Antipas into the territory of Herod Philip to Caesarea Philippi. Here, amid the temples to Caesar, "god" of political and military power, and Pan, god of life and fertility, and the entranceway to Hades and the powers of death, Jesus asks his disciples, "Who do people say that I am?" (Mark 8:27). In response, the disciples recount rumors they have heard. Perhaps John the Baptist risen from the dead? Perhaps Elijah? Perhaps the prophet God promised in Deuteronomy 18:18, who will speak with the authority of Moses? Jesus responds, "And

Caesarea Philippi is where Peter recognized Jesus as the Christ.

> **Some Druze can be distinguished by their black pantaloons and white turbans.**

what about you? Who do you say that I am?" And for once Peter gets it right: "You are the Christ" (Mark 8:29). In Matthew 16:17-20, Jesus answers, "Happy are you, Simon son of Jonah, because no human has shown this to you. Rather my Father who is in heaven has shown this to you. I tell you that you are Peter. And I'll build my church on this rock. The gates of the underworld won't be able to stand against it. I'll give you the keys of the kingdom of heaven."

This concludes the essential elements of your visit to Banias. If time is a constraint, return to the parking lot. But there are other options if time and fortitude allow.

You can follow the upper or lower trails to the west (toward the restrooms) to reach the excavations across the highway and/or the hike to Banias Falls. The upper path is recommended, as it passes beneath the white-domed tomb of the Druze and Muslim saint Nebi Khader. Immediately below the tomb is a large flat rectangle that may have provided the base for Herod Philip's palace. The construction of the wall, with bricks laid at 45-degree angles, is the same architectural technique utilized in Herod the Great's summer palace in Jericho.

Follow the signs, with the help of your national park map-brochure (available at the entrance), to Crusader Banias, or the palace of Agrippa II. Herod Philip's nephew Agrippa I ruled the Golan only four years after his uncle's death in 41 CE, and then the tetrarchy passed to Agrippa's son, who ruled the entire second half of the century. Agrippa II supported Rome in the First Jewish Revolt (66-70 CE), after which Titus paid him the honor of a long visit. Josephus reports that the two enjoyed watching prisoners perish at the mouths of wild animals or in mock combat.[22]

> **The upper path passes beneath the tomb of the Druze and Muslim saint, Nebi Khader.**

If Banias Falls is your destination, follow the signs and

map to the west for about an hour along the Hermon/Banias stream through lovely vegetation and the occasional historical remains. The falls can also be reached by taking the highway a short distance toward Kiryat Shmone and turning left. You will need your receipt to enter, or, alternatively, you can begin at the falls and show your receipt upon entering Banias. (The falls and main site are included under one entrance fee, and both are included on the national park ticket.)

Another option is to descend the same steps you climbed to the cave and Panaeon and then turn to the left, where the trail to the Banias Lookout is marked for a gorgeous view. The physically fit might be tempted to hike the trail all the way to Nimrod's Fortress, which sits perched like a lion upon the adjacent mountain, guarding the pass between Damascus and Banias. This impressive fortress, surrounded as it is with alternating round and square towers, was constructed by the Arabs and Mamluks at the end of the Crusades and named after the legendary hunter of Genesis 10:8-9.[23] If you make the hike, you should have transportation meet you at Nimrod and ample water for the journey. If you do not have time or energy to walk, you can visit the fortress by car or bus via Highway 99 and turning north on Highway 989.

Mount Hermon and the Upper Galilee

The site of the Transfiguration could be Mount Hermon, known in the ancient Near East as Har Tzafon, the mythical mountain of the gods, the peak of which is nine thousand feet above sea level. The traditional veneration of the Transfiguration on Mount Tabor, which is more likely, was a Byzantine decision. Six days after what is generally known as Peter's confession (Mark 8:27–9:1 and parallels), Jesus took Peter, James, and John to the top of a high mountain. Elijah, of course, did not die but was taken by God to heaven, and the mysterious circumstances surrounding Moses' death (Deuteronomy 34:5-6) led to the belief that God had also taken Moses to heaven. Hence the two great

> The designation of Mt. Tabor as the Mount of Transfiguration was made during the Byzantine rule.

Galilee

Mount Hermon

pillars of the Old Testament Law and the Prophets are able to appear with Jesus on the mountain of mystery.

Mount Hermon is actually a small mountain chain, a third of which is shared today by Israel, Syria, and Lebanon. It is visible throughout your drive in the upper Golan. A good place to stop for lunch and pictures is in the Druze village of Masada at Berkat Ram, a natural crater lake at Berkat Ram Kiosk (phone: 04-698-3362; there is sufficient parking for buses). The specialty is a Druze homemade pita spread with lebane and zatar, but falafel and schnitzel are also available. Be sure to try the home-cured olives, perhaps the best in Israel!

The Druze in Israel are congregated in the upper Golan and on Mount Carmel. Their religion, an offshoot of Islam, originated in Egypt in the eleventh century CE, was influenced by Persian mysticism, focuses on the attainment of wisdom, and includes reincarnation into the Druze community. They are a closed society of secret doctrines, and their sages can be distinguished by their black pantaloons and white turbans. They are also a kind and loving people, ready to help the stranger and welcome guests with generosity. Their biblical patron is Moses' father-in-law, Jethro, whom they venerate at a tomb constructed below the Horns of Hattin just west of Tiberias.

Head south on Highway 98 and stop at Kuneitra to observe the U.N. peacekeeping force on the Syrian border and for a good view of Mount Hermon. Looking to the east, the cluster of white buildings immediately before you is the U.N. compound in the "no-man's-land," and beyond that is the Syrian village of Kuneitra.

Gamla (National Park)

As is obvious from its shape, *Gamla* in Hebrew means "camel." It was a city renowned as a Zealot stronghold, even minting coins with the inscription "For the liberation of Jerusalem."[24] Agrippa II, who ruled the Golan from his capital in Caesarea Philippi, sided with the Romans during the First Jewish Revolt (66–70 CE). He besieged Gamla for seven months without success, so, a month later, Vespasian arrived in October of 67 CE with three Roman legions. They managed to breach the wall during their first attack, but the Jews defeated them and inflicted heavy casualties. In November, three legionnairs stealthily removed the supporting stones of the guard tower (visible today from the Gamla lookout), throwing the city into a panic. Titus led the charge, and when it was over, all 9,000 inhabitants were dead—4,000 at the hands of the Romans, and 5,000 following suicidal leaps off the steep cliff into the ravine of the Gamla stream.

Gamla

The national park is also a nature reserve for birds of prey, and it has mounted a colossal effort to save the local griffon vultures from extinction. It is therefore imperative that you walk only on the marked paths, and as in all the national parks, do not touch the flora, so that others may enjoy it after you. The reserve closes its entrance strictly one hour before the park closes, so it is necessary to arrive before 3 p.m. in the winter and before 4 p.m. in the summer.

From the restrooms, walk to the opposite end of the parking lot to begin the short circular trail that takes you to the Gamla Lookout with its explanatory signs and quotes from Josephus. Then continue around the trail to the birds of prey overlook (silence on your walk will increase your chances of seeing these magnificent creatures), from which the Gamla Falls are also visible. At the completion of the circle are the ruins of a Byzantine village with its monastery and unique church. (It has a square apse similar to churches in Syria and Jordan but not otherwise extant in Israel.)

If you have scheduled half a day or more for Gamla, you can take one of the other hiking trails. From the Gamla Lookout, a steep trail descends (and ascends on the way back!) to the Gamla excavations, including the tower, the breach in the wall, the synagogue and mikveh, and olive press and mikveh (since one needed to be ritually pure to process the olive oil). The synagogue is one of the few that were in use concurrently with the Second Temple (though the number is growing due to extensive excavations all over the country). It was after the fall of the Temple that the synagogue movement became the standard for Judaism.

The Dolmen Trail leads to the striking Gamla Falls and takes about an hour and a half round trip. There have been approximately seven hundred dolmens discovered near Gamla and thousands of others throughout the Golan. A dolmen (stone table) comprises two upright monoliths with an additional one placed laterally on top. Our best guess is that they are tombs of nomadic people who traversed the Golan Heights during the early middle Bronze Age, about 2000 BCE.

Katzrin

Also known as: Qasrin

Treat yourself to a delightful and educational visit to the site named the "Talmudic Village of Ancient Katzrin." Many of the places in Israel present only the excavated ruins, but here the site (only 10 percent of which has been uncovered) is reconstructed to show us how Golani Jews of the Byzantine period actually lived (ca. 350–750 CE). If you visited Bet She'arim or Zippori, you may recall that Judah ha-Nasi compiled the Mishnah, or the collection of Jewish oral law, during the Roman period (ca. 200 CE). Then, roughly congruent with what Christians call the Byzantine period, Jewish sages expounded on the Mishnah to produce the Talmud. So Jews refer to this same era as the Talmudic period. I recommend you begin your tour with "The Talmudic Experience," a multimedia drama portraying the world of the Talmud and the minds of the rabbis who produced it. You'll need to arrange this at the entrance when you purchase your ticket. Then work your way back: the restored houses of Uzi and Rabbi Abun, and the synagogue oriented by the basalt bimah that supported the wooden ark facing Jerusalem, and the oil

Katzrin synagogue

Galilee

See how the Jews of the Byzantine period lived at this reconstructed site.

press. Katzrin was devastated by the winter earthquake of 749 CE.

Contact information: Phone: 04-696-2412; website: katzrinp@netvision.net.il. Open Sunday through Thursday, 9a.m.–4p.m.; Friday and eves of holidays, 9 a.m.–2 p.m.; Saturday, 10 a.m.–4 p.m. Buy the full ticket, which includes the Golan Archaeological Museum in the city center of modern Katzrin. The museum includes a three-dimensional audiovisual presentation on Gamla, which is helpful for better understanding the site.

The Golan Heights is home to copious apple and cherry orchards, as well as vineyards. The rich volcanic soil gives the wine made from these grapes a robust flavor. The Golan Heights Winery in modern Katzrin, the economic and cultural center of the Golan, offers tours and some insight into industry in the region. Tours and tasting should be arranged in advance, especially for large groups (phone: 04-696-8435 or 04-696-8409; website: www.golanwines. co.il/en/The-Winery).

Kursi (National Park)

Jesus' healing of the demoniac on the other side of the Sea of Galilee took place in "the region of the Gerasenes" (or the Gadarenes/ Gergesenes; Mark 5:1). Gerasa (Jerash) is thirty-three miles east of the sea, and Gadara is six miles southeast. However, Gergesa (Kursi) was known to rabbinical sources and to the pre-Byzantine sources Origen and Eusebius, so it has more credibility as the actual location. The trail to the site leads you into the church of the large fifth-century CE monastery that provided hospitality to Byzantine pilgrims who flocked to this surprisingly popular destination. Sadly, most of the fauna in the mosaic floor have been obliterated, leaving only flora and geometric designs. (A fortunate bird or two survived; look closely.) The path exiting the church ascends a steep hill to a small chapel on the precipice, which is likely the original fourth-century CE shrine around which the monastery developed.[25]

Cliff of Gergesa on "the Other Side"

Excavations in 2002 revealed evidence of the violent 614 CE Persian invasion, and while the Christian community did return, it was ultimately destroyed by the January earthquake of 749 CE.

Hippos

Also known as: Sussita

The road up to the Decapolis city site of Hippos is, at this writing, closed to the public (but this could change). Academic student groups who have the motivation and energy to walk up the tel on foot should use the following as their guide: Arthur Segal and Michael Eisenberg, "The Spade Hits Sussita," *BAR* 32:3 (May/June 2006): 40–51, 78.

Hippos (Sussita)

Quiet eastern shore

En Gev

Also known as: Ein Gev

If you would like to lodge on the quiet side of the Sea of Galilee, apart from all the hustle and bustle of Tiberias, this is your place (across the street from Hippos). One of Israel's most historic kibbutzim, En Gev offers a guesthouse with options ranging from condos to beachfront bungalows. They also have one of the area's premier fish restaurants and operate sailing opportunities on the Sea of Galilee (see www.eingev.com). Upon request, groups may receive a guided tour of the kibbutz, which includes a history of the kibbutz movement and an immersion in their dairy and agricultural industries.

Hamat Gader

This out-of-the-way site, on the edge of the Golan Heights, the Yarmuk River valley, and the Jordanian border, is an Eden of relaxation. Once the playground of Syrian military officers, it is now the R & R destination for Israeli soldiers. If you have the time to just get away and sit under the soothing waterfalls in the mineral hot springs, do it. The ruins of the Roman

Visit this modern-day Eden for relaxation.

Golan Heights/Jordanian border

baths are also worth a visit, if your scholarly guilt prompts you to do so. There is also a third-century CE Roman theater and a fifth-century CE synagogue.

Bet She'an (National Park)

"Look how the mighty warriors have fallen! Look how the weapons of war have been destroyed!" (2 Samuel 1:27). Thus concludes the most poignant elegy in the Bible: David's lament over the deaths of his mentor, Saul, and his best friend, Jonathan, who perished here at Bet She'an at the hands of the Philistines. This mood is captured atop the tel by the cruciform tree upon which Judas hanged himself in the movie version of *Jesus Christ Superstar*. The tel, which towers over the rest of the ongoing excavations and contains at least fifteen cities layered on top of one another, is the Old Testament site. The Romans named the lower city Scythopolis, and, as huge and impressive as the ruins are, only one-tenth of the metropolis has been unearthed.

Location explains this city's importance. It guards the essential Valley of Jezreel, the artery passing between Galilee and Samaria that connects the Via Maris with Syria and Mesopotamia on its eastern end, parallel to Megiddo, which protected the valley's western extremity. It lies alongside the fecund Harod River, whose gushing waters can be heard on the northern side of the national park. And of course, it is blessed with elevation.

Galilee

Tel Bet She'an

During the Canaanite period (sixteenth–twelfth centuries BCE), Bet She'an was an administrative center of the Egyptian Empire. During the eleventh century BCE, the Philistines managed to migrate up the Via Maris and the Valley of Jezreel to make the city their own. This is why David's elegy says, "Don't talk about it in Gath; don't bring news of it to Ashkelon's streets, or else the Philistines' daughters will rejoice; the daughters of the uncircumcised will celebrate" (2 Samuel 1:20). During the Roman period, Scythopolis was one of the Decapolis cities and not, strictly speaking, part of either Galilee or Samaria. This may account for the absence of its mention in the New Testament. The Byzantine city boasted thirty thousand to forty thousand inhabitants, but after suffering the attack of the Arab conquest, it was destroyed by the dreadful earthquake of 749 CE.

At the park's entrance are restrooms, a gift shop, and a pleasant outdoor café (closed Saturdays), as well as an informative model of the site, which is a good place to begin your tour. Looking toward the tel from here, you see the *cardo maximus*, the heart of every Roman city, usually on a roughly north-south axis. The archaeologists have named it "Palladius Street" after the man mentioned in the sidewalk mosaic. It intersects with the *decumanus* (the essential east-west road in a Roman town), the cross street on an east-west axis, likewise nicknamed "Silvanus Street" after inscriptions found. Descend and turn left into the bathhouse for a self-guided tour, but note that the explanatory signs read right to left like Hebrew! Proceed north on the *cardo* with columns, shops, and sidewalks on either side. (Note that utilitarian Byzantine marble has been laid on top of Roman mosaics.) On your left is a semicircular "mall." Note the stunning mosaic in one of the rooms. It features Tyche, goddess of fortune and patron protector of the city, which crowns her head while she holds a cornucopia of plenty. On your right is the Roman basilica that became the Byzantine agora (market).

When you reach the juncture with the *decumanus*, bear right on "Northern Street" to walk to the top of the tel. You can use the stairs, but you may want to pass the tel and turn left at its base to walk down "Valley Street," which once took citizens north across a bridge over the Harod River to an expansion of the city on the adjacent hill. Archaeologists think there was a hippodrome (Greek stadium) alongside this street (where the palm trees are now planted). At the end of the street, before the bridge, make a sharp turn left to walk up a sheep path to reach the top of the tel. You'll enter through the Crusader gate and adjacent cistern, but it's hard not to imagine the bodies of Saul and Jonathan hanging on the Philistine city wall (1 Samuel 31), where the inhabitants of Jabesh-gilead rescued them and buried them across the Jordan River.

Follow the path up to the Egyptian administrative center, then around to the east (toward the Jordan) for a striking overlook of the Jordan River valley and Gilead on the other side of it. The path turns south back toward the park's entrance. Along the way there are well-marked ruins from various periods. The circular path concludes at a second overlook, this time facing the Roman city. Peer down and you will see the city center, the juncture of the *cardo* and the *decumanus*, with its three imposing structures. The one on the right is a temple, probably dedicated to Dionysus; in the middle is the nymphaeum, or public fountain central to every Roman city; and on the left is a monumental platform. Carefully descend the stairs to exit the tel.

Continue walking east on the *decumanus* toward the park entrance. Walk past the eastern bathhouse, the public toilets, and a sacred compound, into the Roman theater built in the first century CE and renovated in the second. While only the lowest tier of limestone seats remains, there were two more built on the basalt foundation above the first tier, seating seven thousand people. On the Roman principle of one seat per ten citizens, that would place the population of Bet She'an in the first–second centuries CE at seventy thousand. Note that the first row of seats had backs for the "first-class tickets." In front of these seats is the orchestra and the stage. Behind the stage would have been a screen of pillars that helped project the sound from the stage forward to the audience.

Just outside the national park is the Roman amphitheater, or circus, which probably had eleven to thirteen rows of seats accommodating six thousand spectators. Gladiatorial and even more gruesome contests probably took place here.

Galilee

Bet Alfa Synagogue

Bet Alfa Synagogue; Ma'ayan Harod; and Gan HaShlosha (National Parks)

Also known as: Beit Alpha Synagogue; En Harod; and Sachne

In the vicinity of Bet She'an are three sites worth visiting if time allows. Bet Alfa Synagogue is from the sixth century CE, built on the basilica model popular for churches and synagogues during the Byzantine/Talmudic period. It is oriented toward Jerusalem, with its holy arc facing southwest. The video presentation explains everything, but suffice it to say that the mosaic floor is an excellent example of Jewish life blending biblical themes with popular culture to produce, if not an artistic masterpiece, then an endearing piece of folk art. The video also ties the site to Bet She'an and Zippori and thus brings some closure (or introduction) to your tour of the Galilee.

Ma'ayan Harod, which supplied the water for Bet She'an, is famous for its "dog-lapping" narrative in Judges 7. Swimming is popular here in the summer. Also nearby is Gan HaShlosha, where the tepid mineral pools and waterfalls provide a unique and superior bathing experience.

NOTES

NOTES

NOTES

NOTES

Samaria

Samaritan hills as seen from across the Valley of Jezreel

Nablus

Shechem
Also known as: Tel Balata

Nablus, the Arabic translation of the Roman *Neapolis* (New City), is the main town of the district of Samaria today. It played a central role during the periods of the patriarchs, the judges, and the early monarchy of the Northern Kingdom of Israel. Its ancient name was Shechem, and it is nestled in the valley between Mount Gerizim and Mount Ebal. In the middle Bronze Age, Abraham passed through here (Genesis 12:6), and under Joshua's leadership it became a major center of liturgical renewal (Joshua 8:30-33; 24). Then, after Solomon's death and the ensuing civil war, Jeroboam made it the capital of his kingdom.

The modern residents of Nablus are extremely gracious and hospitable, even given the adversities they have suffered since 1948; and Palestinians generally recognize the olive oil from Nablus as the best in the region. The most interesting find at Shechem is the

Shechem

Samaria

platform of the temple of Ba'al (El) Berit (Lord of the Covenant), with an altar and *matsevah* (large standing stone marking holy space in the ancient Near East), which were in use during the late Bronze Age (Canaanite period) but destroyed and built over during the early Iron Age (Israelite period).[26]

Jacob's Well

Located on the eastern outskirts of Nablus, this well (Genesis 33:18-20; John 4), which is more than one hundred feet deep and in antiquity was much deeper, has some claim to authenticity since a well is somewhat of an anomaly in a region with so many springs. Already in 333 CE, the Bordeaux pilgrim mentions a baptistery over the well, and by about 380, a cruciform church had been constructed around it. The Crusaders rebuilt the church, and the crypt

A priest at Jacob's well

of the modern church, finished in 2007, was part of the Crusader church.

Mount Gerizim

The Samaritans continue unto today, most of them living on their sacred mountain, Mount Gerizim, as referenced by the statement to Jesus by the Samaritan woman at Jacob's well: "Our ancestors worshipped on this mountain, but you and your people say that it is necessary to worship in Jerusalem" (John 4:20). The archaeological evidence suggests there was a Samaritan temple atop Mount Gerizim already in the fifth century BCE, probably predating Nehemiah's arrival in Jerusalem in 445 BCE (see www. biblicalarchaeology.org/uncategorized/magens-response/).[27]

The remains you will view today, covering a broad area, are from the second Samaritan temple built about 200 BCE. There are stairs to ascend the holy area, which was surrounded by gates and towers. The two spots within this area revered by the Samaritans today are the "Twelve Stones" (Joshua 4:1-9), located along the northwest wall; and the "Summit of the World," the fenced flat rock (near the parking lot) used originally for the Samaritan Passover sacrifices, which continue to this day, although lower on the mountain. The

Samaria

Ruins on Mount Gerizim, with Mount Ebal in the background

> **Mount Gerizim is sacred to Samaritans even today.**

Samaritans, like the Jewish Sadducees of Jesus' day, accept only the five books of Moses as inspired scripture.

In the center of the ruins of the Samaritan temple, just east of the "Twelve Stones," are the remains of an octagonal fifth-century CE Byzantine church dedicated to Mary the mother of God (*Theotokos*), surrounded by a rectangular fortified wall (which sits within the excavated walls of the Samaritan temple). On the northern ridge of Mount Gerizim (Tel er-Ras) are the remains of a second-century CE Roman temple dedicated to Zeus, which was pictured on the coins of Neapolis (Nablus).

Samaria (National Park)
Also known as: Sabaste

King Omri founded Samaria in 876 BCE (1 Kings 16:24) on a high hill northwest of Shechem. His son Ahab continued to build the capital, but Ahab's wife, Jezebel, princess of Tyre, brought her

Samaria/Sabaste

foreign religious practices with her to Samaria. This provoked criticism from the prophet Elijah. Under King Jeroboam II (784–748 BCE), Samaria prospered but also became the center of a powerful and oppressive aristocracy that prompted the prophets Amos, Hosea, Micah, and Isaiah to predict her destruction. This occurred at the hands of the Assyrians (724–722 BCE), who deported about thirty thousand Israelites and replaced them with foreigners. During the Persian period, Samaria was a provincial capital that, with Alexander the Great's conquest in 333–331 BCE, became a Greek city, itself destroyed by the Hasmonean John Hyrcanus in 108 BCE. In 30 BCE, Caesar Augustus gave Samaria to Herod the Great, who rebuilt it into a fine city once more and named it Sebaste in honor of Caesar (in Greek, *Sebastos* = Augustus). The Romans destroyed Sebaste during the First Jewish Revolt (66–70 CE), and it became a Roman colony in 200 CE.

As you approach the tel on the road from the west, you will first meet the Greco-Roman ruins of the city gate and wall. Pass through them, and you will see the Roman-columned street to the right of the road. Once you reach the parking lot, you will see what remains of the columns that surrounded the rectangular Roman forum with the basilica on its western end, opposite the modern restaurant and restrooms, which are adjacent to a raised overlook. From there to the north you can view the long, rectangular stadium that was within the walls of the Roman city. Walk west up the path in front of the restaurant to view the Roman theater. Then continue up to the acropolis, passing the round Hellenistic tower that breaches the ancient Israelite wall.

Atop the acropolis are steps, currently in their Roman modification, that were once crowned by the temple Herod dedicated to Augustus. Pass the steps and turn left to admire the finely constructed wall of the Omri-Ahab palace, parallel to the path running along the western side of the acropolis. The ruins higher up, adjacent to the Temple of Augustus, are Herodian. Continue southward on the path for a magnificent view of the Ephraimite hill country. (If you can arrange to be here at sunset, it is a real treat!)

As you reach the end of the circuit, you will find yourself in a small church from the Byzantine and Crusader periods. Perhaps because Herod the Great celebrated a marriage feast here, and also murdered two of his sons here, Christian legend connected the site to the beheading of John the Baptist by Herod Antipas (Herod the Great's son). Just before ending at the parking lot, note another part of the Omri-Ahab wall visible just south of the Roman basilica. East of the parking lot is the Crusader cathedral of John the Baptist, built over what they claimed to be his tomb, now a mosque.

NOTES

NOTES

Judea

Armenian procession through the Old City

Judea

Jerusalem

An excellent place to lodge during your stay in the Holy City is the Olive Tree Hotel, 23 St. George Street, located just north of the Damascus Gate and voted the best hotel in Jerusalem (www. olivetreehotel.com). It is in a mixed Arab-Jewish neighborhood, and it's only a ten- or fifteen-minute walk to the Old City (Damascus Gate to the Muslim Quarter and New Gate into the Christian Quarter). The hotel is also on the city train line, which connects to bus routes all over the new city, and is situated at the head of a major shopping street (Salahadin). There is also a medical clinic right across the street, and the Rockefeller Archaeological Museum is just up the road. The nearby Hebrew University gym and swimming pool are available for your use free of charge. Also across the street is St. George Cathedral (Anglican), which welcomes worshipers of all denominations; worship times every day of the week can be viewed at www.j-diocese.org.

City of David

City of David

This elongated plateau, comprising the original Jerusalem, makes its first appearance in the Bible in Genesis 14:18 (called Shalem/Salem), where Abraham meets King Melchizedek, high priest of El Elyon (God Most High). *Jerusalem* (Jeru-shalem) could mean "secure foundation," though this is debated by linguists. Even so, it certainly was a secure foundation. The plateau is surrounded by the Kidron Valley (on the east) and the Central/Tyropoean Valley (on the west), which were much deeper in ancient times than they are today. King Hezekiah filled in the Central Valley in the eighth century BCE when his city expanded to the west; and sediment and debris of millennia have taken their toll on the secure depth of the Kidron. At any rate, what a fortified city needed in antiquity was natural height, a defensive wall, and a constant water supply (the Gihon Spring). Ancient Jerusalem had all three.[28]

So strong was Canaanite (Jebusite) Jerusalem that it was not taken by Joshua or Saul, and the task was left to David. He accomplished this feat by infiltrating the city's waterworks from the Gihon Spring in the Kidron Valley into the interior of the city. Centrally located and not the possession of any Israelite tribe, it was the ideal choice for his emerging kingdom's capital, which he renamed the

> Ancient Jerusalem was well defended with a commanding view, defensive wall, and dependable water supply.

"City of David." He built his palace and brought the ark of the covenant here to solidify religion and government.

Information about the site can be found at www.cityofdavid.org.il/en. Opening hours in winter: Sunday–Thursday, 8 a.m.–5 p.m.; Friday, 8 a.m.–2 p.m.; in summer: Sunday–Thursday, 8 a.m.–7 p.m.; Friday, 8 a.m.–4 p.m.; closed Shabbat. Holiday eve closing times are listed on the website. The entrance to Hezekiah's Tunnel is locked one hour before closing times. Reservations are required for groups. Enter from the road along the now-filled-in Central (Tyropoean) Valley on the northwestern edge of the plateau (just across the street and down from the Dung Gate). Guided tours are available (check at the ticket counter for times/languages) but not necessary if your group has a guide/teacher; or, if you are on your own, you don't mind using the very thorough park brochure. Also see www.alt-arch.org for a very helpful introduction to the city of Jerusalem and the City of David, and the highly contested nature of the excavations in this area. Begin your walking tour with the 3-D movie, and then walk up the stairs immediately to the left of the theater exit for a spectacular overlook. To your left is the Temple Mount, and before you is the Kidron Valley with the Mount of Olives hovering above it. You can see the myriad "whitewashed tombs" of which Jesus spoke (Matthew 23:27), and the Garden of Gethsemane, topped by the golden onion domes of the St. Mary Magdalene Russian Orthodox convent. Descend the stairs and retrace your steps back down the sidewalk; then proceed to the stairwell descending to the archaeological excavations.

Go down the stairs to view what archaeologist Eilat Mazar believes to be the foundation of David's palace, based on its palatial dimension, concurrence with biblical location, and carbon 12 and pottery dating to the tenth century BCE. This area must have still been part of the royal establishment in the seventh century BCE as two *bullae* (clay seals for rolled documents with the impressed signatures of royal officials) were found here with the names of court officials hostile to the prophet Jeremiah (Jeremiah 38:1, 4).

Judea

Continue walking down the next flight of stairs to the royal quarter excavated by Kathleen Kenyon. Standing or sitting at the observation platform, straight ahead and up, you will see the glacis (stepped-stone structure) that

> **Could this be the remains of King David's palace?**

may have originally supported the Jebusite citadel and then subsequently David's palace. Just beneath it in this upper-class neighborhood, you will see the "House of Ahiel" whose name was found on a potsherd within it. It is a good example of the typical Israelite four-room house. Behind the two pillars still standing was a room, in front of them an open courtyard, and in front of that another roofed room. To the right was the "fourth room," probably with two stories. Proof that it was a wealthy family is their own toilet seat just to the right.

This house and the adjacent one were burned, along with this entire royal quarter, by the Babylonian invasion in 586 BCE (2 Kings 25:8-9), as evidenced by the thick layer of ash, piles of debris, numerous arrowheads, and charred wooden furniture imported from Syria. Just above the stepped-stone structure and to the right are the remains of Nehemiah's wall, which he built around Jerusalem when he returned from Babylon with Ezra the priest in the mid-fifth century BCE. Note that it was constructed farther up the slope than the previous walls, probably because he was able to construct it higher upon the debris of the Babylonian destruction (Nehemiah 3:31-32).

Continue forward (to your left as you face the stone glacis) and up the path to a lovely overlook of the Arab village of Silwan across the Kidron Valley. If you look carefully on the lower levels among the houses, you can see some of the fifty or so burial caves from Jerusalem's cemetery for the wealthy during the First Temple period. One of them bears the inscription of Shebna/Shebniahu, mentioned in Isaiah 22:15-16, whom the prophet criticized for his tomb's arrogant opulence. If you look carefully midway up the mount and to your left, you will see, freestanding and hewn out of the rock hillside, a magnificent square tomb topped by a "crown molding" that originally

> **Some ancient wealthy families had indoor plumbing.**

supported a pyramid (sadly quarried away by later inhabitants). This tomb dates perhaps from the time of Hezekiah (eighth century BCE), when Egyptian influence was strong in Judah (Isaiah 30:1-5; 31:1-3; though it could also date from the seventh century BCE). Popularly called the "Tomb of Pharaoh's Daughter" (1 Kings 9:16-17), it was actually the funerary monument of "a prominent public figure, obviously one of the leading officials of the Kingdom of Judah in the late First Temple period."[29]

Proceed on the walking path down many stairs until, on your right, you see the sign marking a sharp right turn into the entrance to Warren's Shaft. If you wish and have the time, you can walk farther down the path until it makes a sharp dogleg turn to the left. Stop there and face the City of David. Immediately before you is what Kathleen Kenyon identified as the foundation of the original Jebusite city gate. She identified the stones just behind it as Hezekiah's wall (the small stones behind that are part of Miss Kenyon's retaining wall). If you took this little excursion, return now to the entrance to Warren's Shaft (named after its discoverer in 1867, British captain Charles Warren).

In the eighteenth century BCE, the Canaanites built the secret tunnel through which you are now descending in order to reach the huge and massively fortified pool they hewed out of the rock near the Gihon Spring just outside the city. In this way, the water supply for the city was accessible from inside the city even if it were besieged; not to mention the obvious advantage over women having to exit the city gate every morning to draw the day's water, even in peacetime. This is probably the way David's soldiers snuck into the city Trojan horse–style to surprise the Jebusites, enabling David to seize Jerusalem for his capital.

At the bottom of the secret tunnel, just before you pass through a small aperture, is a lighted shaft descending to your left. This is Warren's Shaft, and for many years it was identified as the "gutter" through which David's soldiers penetrated this lofty walled city.

> This secret tunnel ensured the city's water supply.

However, if you examine carefully the sides of the tunnel as you descend, you will see a horizontal line in the stone about half way up, marking from where the tunnel floor was lowered in the eighth century BCE, which exposed Warren's Shaft for the first time—nothing more than a natural karstic hole in the rock.

Passing through the aperture, the great pool is on your right as you enter the large underground room. As you turn left on to the metal platform, the pool's fortifications are in front of you. The foundations of the spring tower that surrounded the Gihon Spring, each stone of which weighs several tons, are beneath your feet. Clearly these ancient Canaanites were fine engineers. Continue descending to the entrance to the Gihon Spring.

It should be clear by now that Jerusalem's success through the millennia was based on not only its natural mountain height but also its secured water supply that originated down in the Kidron Valley. By the eighth century BCE, the Judean city had spread to the west across the Central Valley and beyond. King Hezekiah built a new wall around this expanded city (part of which can be seen in the current Jewish Quarter of the Old City). He also had his engineers hew a tunnel from the Gihon Spring under the City of David to bring water farther west into the city. These actions may have been precipitated by an encroaching threat of Assyrian invasion. The tunnel is about 1,750 feet long, and if walkers scrutinize the left wall about twenty feet before the end, they can see where the Siloam inscription had been, describing how the engineers hewed from both ends and met at this spot.

Gihon means "gushing," and the depth of the water in the tunnel is unpredictable. Generally, it is between knee- and waist-level high. You must have a flashlight and something on your feet. I recommend you wear a bathing suit under your street clothes, which you can shed before stepping into the wet tunnel and carry with you in a light backpack. You will exit at the Siloam Spring, and the walk is about half an hour depending on how fast you walk and the volume of traffic in the tunnel. Should you not wish to get wet, at the same entrance to the Gihon Spring is a Canaanite tunnel that was literally left high and dry when Hezekiah dug his deeper tunnel to the west. The part of this tunnel that is walkable is lit, a five- to ten-minute walk, and will deposit you outside in roughly the middle of the City of David.

From there you have three options. You can walk up the hill, turn right past the entrance to Warren's Shaft, and walk all the way up back to your original entrance into the City of David (where you bought your ticket and saw the movie). Or, upon exiting the dry tunnel, you can make a sharp left and walk out the exit gate into the Kidron Valley. Turn right and follow the street to the southern tip of the City of David, where you can enter the Siloam Pool excavations on your right. (Your ticket stub from Warren's Shaft will get you in.)

The third option is the most interesting, but it is a moderately difficult walk over some rocks. Upon exiting the dry tunnel, walk up the hill as in the first option, but at the top of the hill turn left rather than right and follow the long path southward until you find yourself on top of what is likely the royal cemetery of the Davidic dynasty, perhaps even David's tomb itself.[30] Unfortunately, this area was heavily quarried by Hadrian in order to build his Aelia Capitolina after 135 CE, and a synagogue actually stood near this spot in the first century CE. Similar to the way other First Temple tombs across the Kidron Valley in Silwan now serve as rooms or basements beneath Palestinian homes, these royal tombs underwent reuse, perhaps as basements or cisterns, during the late Second Temple period when memory of their original significance had faded.

The most imposing tomb, called T1,[31] is the one farthest to the west next to the modern stone wall. It is similar in its simplicity to other late Bronze Age/early Iron Age tombs, such as that of Ahiram, Phoenician king of Byblos, who may have been a contemporary of David. In the upper rear chamber is carved a six by four foot depression that may have held a sarcophagus (as did Ahiram's tomb). At some point the floor immediately in front of this chamber was lowered and an artificial floor inserted into the grooves on either side, making a two-storied tomb (room for more kings of Judah?). A new doorway and stairs were also cut into the rock at the far end of the tunnel to provide entryway to the lower level. Archaeologists have long wondered why King Hezekiah's engineers dug their tunnel in an indirect route south through the Kidron Valley and cut it sharply to the west only at the southern tip of the City of David. The most logical explanation is that they wanted to avoid disturbing the Royal Necropolis by carving out Hezekiah's Tunnel around it rather than going through it.

Continue walking past the Meyuhas House down the path to the "Three Valleys Lookout" to view the convergence of the Kidron with the Central and the Hinnom Valleys going off to the west. The natural amphitheater before you is called En Rogel, where Adonijah tried to have himself made king instead of Solomon while David was up in his palace on his deathbed (1 Kings 1). Walk farther down to the end of the path to turn right into the entrance gate to the Siloam Pool excavations.

The stepped pool, found in 2004, dates to the New Testament period, and is therefore the one where Jesus healed the man born blind. After rubbing mud he made with his own saliva into the man's eyes, Jesus told the man to wash in the Pool of Siloam (*Shiloah* in Hebrew; *Silwan* in Arabic). The upper pool at the outlet of Hezekiah's Tunnel is Byzantine and was originally connected to a church that was later replaced with the mosque.

Judea

Temple Mount entrance

Temple Mount

Also known as: Har Ha-Bayit;
Haram esh-Sharif (The Noble
Sanctuary)

The Temple Mount is holy to Jews, Christians, and Muslims.

The opening hours at the Temple Mount vary along with political fluctuations. Generally count on Sunday–Thursday, 8 a.m.–10 a.m., possibly also 12:30 p.m.–1:30 p.m. There could be somewhat later hours during the summer. Closed Friday and Shabbat. It is best to go first thing in the morning and get in line early—the line farthest to the right. The other lines go only to the Western Wall below and not to the Temple Mount above. You may not enter with Bibles or anything that looks like a holy book. Be warned, they will be confiscated. As everywhere in the Old City, travel light (a very small backpack or no bag at all) due to security checks.

Entering the Temple Mount plaza, proceed straight to stand in front of the El-Aksa Mosque with the black dome. Note the stairway ascending from below. This is where the New Testament Temple stairs brought pilgrims, such as Jesus and his family, from the mikvehs below into the holy area of the Temple Mount. There was a second stairway to the left that is now off-limits to non-Muslims.

Solomon had built his palace just above his father David's, between the City of David and the El-Aksa Mosque, roughly where the modern street is today. Herod built his apartments where this mosque stands today, and below them the Royal Portico, a popular gathering place for rabbis to discuss theology and the interpretation of Torah. El-Aksa, short for *masjid el-aksa* (the furthermost sanctuary), originally referred to the entire Temple Mount as the spot Islam located Muhammad's Night Journey and ascent into heaven where he received, among other things, instructions from God that Muslims should pray five times a day. Built by Umayyad caliphs in 709–715 CE over Herod's artificial extension of Mount Zion's southern end, this mosque was destroyed twice by earthquakes. When the Crusaders came in 1099 CE, it became first the palace of the king of

Judea

> **Solomon's Temple was built on the site where Abraham went to sacrifice Isaac.**

Jerusalem and then the residence of the soldier-monks, Templars.

Turn now to face the golden dome and walk up to it. This older mosque is built over a very large flat rock that was probably the threshing floor of Araunah, upon which David constructed an altar and offered sacrifice (2 Samuel 24). Threshing floors were sacred spaces in the ancient world, and this one was likely the center of the cult of El Elyon, Most High God (see Genesis 14 and above), which David allowed to be absorbed into the worship of the God of Sinai.[32]

Here Solomon built the Temple, and 2 Chronicles 3:1 identifies it as Mount Moriah, where the binding of Isaac occurred (Genesis 22).[33] The first Temple was destroyed by the Babylonians in 586 BCE and then rebuilt under the auspices of prophets Haggai and Zechariah by 516 BCE. Herod expanded the Temple Mount with immense retaining walls, fill, and arched supports, so strong that the dimensions of the current esplanade are Herodian. A two-meter-high fence separated the holy area from the Court of the Gentiles, and at each of its thirteen gates was written in Greek or Latin, "No Gentile to enter the fence and barrier around the Temple. Anyone caught is answerable to himself for the ensuing death." This is the "barrier of hatred" broken down by Christ in Ephesians 2:14. Inside the wall were designated degrees of holiness. First there was the Court of the Women. Then was the Court of the Priests, where the worship services took place around the altar. After that, only priests could enter the Temple building, and only the high priest could enter the holy of holies one day a year, on Yom Kippur (the Day of Atonement).

Byzantine Christians considered the Temple Mount accursed and used it for a quarry, but when Caliph Omar took the city in 638 CE, he built a crude mosque in the temple esplanade. Umayyad caliphs built the Dome of the Rock mosque during the period of 688–691 CE and denied access to non-Muslims. The Crusaders converted it into a church that they called "the Temple of the Lord," but

Saladin in 1187 CE had only to remove the altar to revert it to a mosque. The current Haram Wall was renewed by Suliman the Magnificent in the six-teenth century CE at the same time that he constructed the current Old City walls.

> **Byzantine Christians thought the Temple Mount was cursed.**

The Dome of the Rock is the first major sanctuary built by Islam and the only one to have survived essentially intact. The builder was Umayyad caliph Abd al-Malik, who concentrated on a mathematical rhythm so that all critical dimensions related to the center circle circumscribing the threshing floor of Araunah (up and around). He wanted to usurp Judaism by claiming the Temple spot, and to usurp Christianity by surpassing the beauty of the jewels and diadems worn by Byzantine rulers in their medallions of Christ and the Virgin. The interior, exe-cuted by Syrian Christians, is meant to evoke the Garden of Eden, or Paradise, but according to Islamic law uses no animal or human figures but only vegetation and Arabic.[34]

The founding inscription is a single line of script running along the top of both sides of the inner octagon, which reads in part, "O you People of the Book, overstep not bounds in your religion, and of God speak only the truth. The Messiah, Jesus, son of Mary, is only an apostle of God, and his Word which he conveyed unto Mary and a Spirit proceeding from him. Believe therefore in God and his apostles, and say not Three. It will be better for you. God is only one God. Far be it from his glory that he should have a son." While this is a rather harsh indictment of Christianity, we should remember that Muslims believe that when Jesus returns he will be the Messiah. They also believe in the miracles of the New Testament such as the virgin birth and the resurrection of Lazarus. Muhammad just could not accept what Paul calls the "scandal" of the cross (1 Corinthians 1:23), so Islam assumes God took Jesus to heaven, like Elijah, and substituted another man to die on the cross.

Walk east down toward the Kidron Valley and the Mount of Olives and turn left to pass the interior of the Golden Gate, double arched and sealed from the outside. There appears to be an arched

Judea

> King Herod believed any uprising would begin here on the Temple Mount.

structure, perhaps Herodian, beneath the current Muslim one, but excavation is impossible due to the sanctity of the Temple Mount/Haram and the Muslim cemetery surrounding the gate. There is also confusion about the name. This may have been the Gate Beautiful, which in Greek is *horaia*; and the Crusaders may have confused it with the Latin *aurea*, meaning "golden." At any rate, the early Byzantine Christians ascribed it (if it existed) no credence whatsoever, assuming that Jesus arrived on Palm Sunday through what today we call the Saint Stephen's/Lions' Gate just north of the Temple Mount.

As you make your way back across the Temple Mount plaza toward the west to exit, look to the far northwest corner to the tall minaret that is today part of a Muslim school. This is where Herod built Antonio Fortress to house a Roman garrison, because any messianic uprising (any rebellion against Roman rule) was sure to be religiously motivated and therefore to begin here. Walk to the western side of the esplanade just past the Dome of the Rock, and exit through the Chain Gate. Follow the signs to the Kotel or the Western Wall.

★ Western Wall
Also known as: HaKotel HaMa'aravi

The Romans destroyed Herod's Temple, fulfilling Jesus' prophecy that not one stone would be left upon another (Matthew 24:2). But the western bottom of Herod's retaining wall that surrounded the Temple esplanade survived as the holiest place in Judaism. The huge beveled stones are Herodian, and they extend well beneath the current ground level. The medium-sized stones are Umayyad from the seventh century CE, and the small stones at the top were a restoration after the earthquake of 1033 CE. You are looking at only one-eighth of the entire Western Wall (180 feet). This part is hallowed because it was the only area aboveground until Israel gained control of East Jerusalem in 1967. To the right (south), another 270 feet is now visible at the Temple Mount Excavations of the Davidson

Western Wall

Center (see below). To the left (north), another 1,000 feet can be visited through the Western Wall tunnels beneath the Muslim Quarter.

Inside the synagogue, Wilson's Arch is visible, which supported an entryway into the Temple Mount from the upper city at the time of Jesus. At the far right end of the women's section, just abutting the right-hand wall, is a barely visible lintel of Barclay's Gate, which served the same purpose.[35] It is traditional to write a prayer on a small slip of paper and place it into a crack in the wall. Neither writing nor photography is allowed in the Western Wall Plaza on Shabbat due to Jewish law. For information and reservations for Western Wall tunnel tours, call 1-599-515-888; and for further information, visit www.thekotel.org.

Temple Mount Excavations
Also known as: Davidson Center

Exit the Western Wall (if you are facing it at the Israeli flag, turn right and walk through the exit gate). Turn right again, walking down toward the Dung Gate, but before you reach the gate, turn right to enter the Davidson Center, which is open Sunday–Thursday, 8 a.m.–5 p.m.; Friday and holiday eves, 8 a.m.–2 p.m.; closed Shabbat. The ticket booth and restrooms are at the entrance, where

Judea

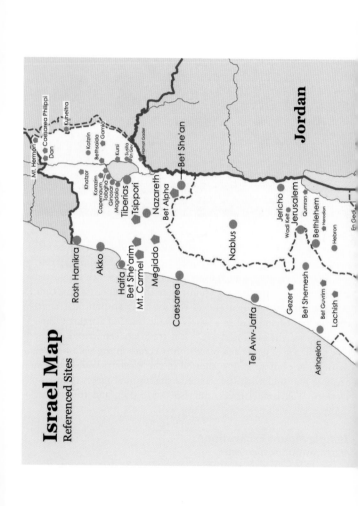

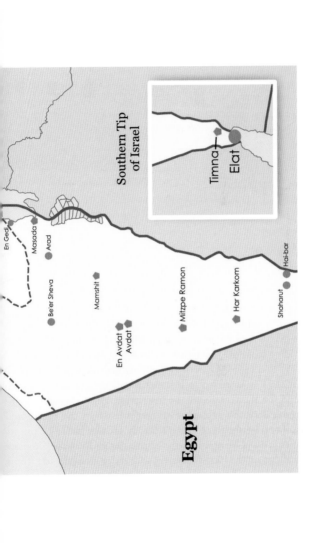

Teaching Steps

you should note the instructive time line on the right-hand wall. From the entry hall, turn right again and walk up to the museum/ theater building. Enter and enjoy the archaeological movie before proceeding to the video about Jewish pilgrimage to the Temple Mount at the time of Jesus (shown in both Hebrew and English).

Exit to the left and climb the stairs, then turn left and walk to the overlook of Robinson's[36] Arch, the butt of which can be seen protruding from the Western Wall corner. It adorned an L-shaped stairway that may have been Herod's own entrance to the Temple Mount since it ascended to his apartments on the southern end. Descend the stairs and note the inscription "To the place of trumpeting [declare the Sabbath/distinguish between the sacred and the profane]," referring to where the shofar was blown by priests to announce commencement and conclusion of Shabbat.[37] You are now walking on the Herodian street with shops along the left (think money changers, sellers of sacrificial animals—as portrayed in the video you just viewed). Jesus and his disciples would most assuredly have walked this street. Note how the huge Herodian stones still lie today where they fell in 70 CE. You can see how far all of this street was underground before the post-1967 Israeli excavations by casting your gaze north to the peninsula of high earth

Jesus as a boy would have ascended these steps with his parents for Passover.

artificially separating the hallowed Western Wall from where you are now standing.[38] Proceed toward that protruding embankment and ascend the stairs for a good overlook of the area, and walk around the catwalk. Then descend carefully to view and enter some of the many mikvehs (ritual baths) that surrounded the Temple Mount (again, recall the video presentation of the Jewish pilgrim from Galilee). Return to the fallen inscription ("To the place of the trumpeting"), pass it to the left, and turn right through the opening. Go forward and turn left through the screen-shaded archaeological plaza through another opening, and before you on the left will lie "the Teaching Steps," just below and south outside the Royal Portico (beneath today's El-Aksa's black-domed mosque). Jesus as a boy would have ascended these steps with his parents for Passover (Luke 2:41-51); and here, as a rabbi, he entered to teach (John 10:22-39).

At the top of the stairs to the west and to the east are the Hulda Gates used by pilgrims. The Double Gate was to the left, but only the view of the far right side of the right-hand gate is not currently obscured by a medieval tower. The Triple Gate, blocked in the eleventh century CE and visible to the right, is Umayyad but in the same place as its Herodian predecessor. In between the two Hulda Gates, just east of the Teaching Steps, were two buildings: the first a bathhouse with mikvehs, the ritual baths required of Jewish pilgrims before they entered the Temple Mount; and the second a law court.[39]

Descend carefully by the modern stairs down to the street that separates the Temple Mount excavations from the City of David. Here archaeologist Eilat Mazar believes she found a portion of King Solomon's city wall, well marked and annotated for a productive self-guided tour. Head back up toward the visitors' center and follow the sign to exit the Davidson Center at the outside rotary gate up at the far left. The Dung Gate of the Old City walls will be to your left, and the way to return to the Western Wall or Jewish Quarter will be to your right. The stairs ascending above the entrance to the Davidson Center

Judea

will take you to the upper Jewish Quarter where there are great places to eat and shop, as well as stimulating archaeological discoveries.

Hurva Synagogue

Jewish Quarter of the Old City

The Jewish Quarter was almost totally destroyed by the Arab-Israeli war of 1948, enabling its archaeological excavation and then modern rebuilding when Israel took control of the Old City after the Six-Day War of 1967. If your last stop was the Western Wall, ascend one of the sets of stairs at the far western end of the Western Wall Plaza. If you have not been here before, it is probably best to continue walking to the far western end of the upper Jewish Quarter to orient yourself at the *cardo*, which has been reconverted into its original function: a vibrant shopping mall. The northern end of the *cardo* was the Crusader market, and the southern end was the Byzantine *cardo maximus*, within which you can view a replica of the fifth-century CE Madaba map of Jerusalem.[40]

Just to the east of the Crusader market, near the juncture of Jewish Quarter Road and Plugat HaKotel, is the Information Office (open 10 a.m.–4:30 p.m.; closed Shabbat along with the rest of the Jewish Quarter), as well as public restrooms. You will also find the Broad Wall here, which was built by King Hezekiah in the eighth century BCE, along with Hezekiah's Tunnel, as part of his attempt to absorb the considerable western expansion of Jerusalem. Just a little farther, where Plugat HaKotel meets Shonei Halachot at Bonei Hahoma Street, is the Rachel Yanait Ben-Zvi Center, which offers guided tours of its model of Old Testament Jerusalem. Open Sunday–Thursday, 9 a.m.–4 p.m.; call 02-628-6288, or ask at the information office for tour times and reservations.

Just to the east of the Byzantine *cardo maximus* is the impressive Hurva Synagogue, destroyed in 1948 CE and recently reconstructed. Tours of the synagogue are by advance reservation only; to reserve, call 02-626-5922, or you can purchase tickets and learn the times of the guided tours at the information office mentioned above. Continuing farther east, back toward the Western Wall/HaKotel, you will find yourself in the expansive and lovely Hurva Square. At its opposite end is the Wohl Archaeological Museum with its superb excavations of Herodian-era mansions. This upper city was definitely upper class, probably largely priestly/Sadducean, with its own entrances into the Temple Mount.

Across the square to the left, at the intersection of Tiferet Israel, is a biblical/Judaica book shop called Shorashim (Roots) whose modern Orthodox Jewish owners, brothers Moshe and Dov Kempinski, will be happy to close their doors if you have a group of students, pull out the chairs, and engage with you in a discussion of Judaism and Jewish-Christian dialogue (phone: 02-628-9729; reservations not required). Farther down Tiferet Israel is the Burnt House, preserved exactly as it was found after being burned in 70 CE by the Romans. This is actually only the basement of a much larger house. A stone weight found therein identifies the owner as Bar Kathros, son of Kathros, known from the Talmud to be a high priestly family. A joint ticket can be purchased for both the Burnt House and the Wohl Archaeological Museum.

Armenian Quarter of the Old City

Armenia, adjacent to Turkey and below Russia, had converted to Christianity before the end of the third century CE and was the first nation to do so. The Armenian Quarter can be reached through either Zion Gate or Jaffa Gate; or, from the Jewish Quarter, by walking up Or Ha-Haim Street just above the open excavations of the

Sign at entrance

cardo maximus to St. James Street, which will take you to Armenian Orthodox Patriarchate Road. Along the way you can turn right on Ararat Street to visit the Syrian Orthodox Church of St. James. On Armenian Orthodox Patriarchate Road, to the left, is the Armenian Cathedral of St. James and adjacent monastery, as well as a wonderful restaurant called the Armenian Tavern.

In the area from roughly the Armenian Tavern to the citadel of Jaffa Gate stood Herod's palace, which became the praetorium (Matthew 27:27; Mark 15:16) of the Roman procurator after Herod's son Archelaus fell out of favor with the Romans in 6 CE. This is where Jesus was tried by Pontius Pilate and marched out the Garden Gate to Golgotha, currently the Church of the Holy Sepulcher, where lay the garden cemetery mentioned by the Gospel of John: "There was a garden in the place where Jesus was crucified" (John 19:41). It is confusing to modern pilgrims that while the Holy Sepulcher is inside the modern sixteenth-century CE walls, it was outside the city walls at the time of Jesus'

> **Armenia was the first nation to convert to Christianity.**

> There is reasonable certainty about where Jesus was buried.

trial, ca. 30 CE. So if you want to walk the "way of the cross," begin at the Armenian Tavern and go right past Jaffa Gate. Turn right down David Street, then left on Christian Quarter Road. Continue until you see on your right the "Mosque of Omar," and make a sharp right into the plaza of the hallowed Church of the Holy Sepulcher.

Why are we pretty sure this was where Jesus was buried? First, we have Josephus's description of the Garden Gate nearby.[41] We have the early Byzantine tradition that Jesus was flogged near the current Zion Gate of the south Armenian Quarter (site of the praetorium). We know that beneath the Holy Sepulcher Church was a limestone rock quarry, which when it was abandoned left an unusable flinty hill. We also know that abandoned quarries in the ancient Mideast often became cemeteries, due to the ease of chiseling tombs into the sides of their soft limestone walls. This is where Joseph of Arimathea dug his unique one-man tomb that he bequeathed to our Lord Jesus. This is why, in the Church of the Holy Sepulcher, the tomb is so close to Golgotha—indeed, under the roof of one church, as currently defined.

The modern Via Dolorosa was created by the Crusaders, who brought the fourteen Stations of the Cross from Roman Catholic Europe. They assumed that the *Lithostratos* beneath the Sisters of Zion convent was the pavement of Antonio Fortress, which they mistakenly thought was the praetorium where Jesus was tried. That stone pavement, however, is dated by archaeologists to Hadrian's reconstruction of the city (135 CE).

⭐ Holy Sepulcher Church

The walk from the praetorium to Golgotha and the Tomb of Christ takes you from the Armenian Quarter to the Christian Quarter, the heart of which is the Church of the Holy Sepulcher. The early Jerusalem Christian community never lost memory of where our Lord was crucified and buried. I have mentioned elsewhere in this book not to confuse the current sixteenth-century

Judea

Syrian Orthodox chapel

CE Old City walls with the biblical walls of Jerusalem. In the 30s CE, when Jesus was tried and crucified by Pontius Pilate (Roman procurator of Judea, 26–36 CE), this spot lay outside the city wall. (Jews at the time would not place a cemetery inside the Holy City's walls.) It was just outside an exit gate (the Garden Gate, see above) so that the Roman spectacle of crucifixion would be seen as an example to all passersby leaving the city for the substantial suburbs that were developing west of the city wall. Liturgical celebrations were held at this site until 66 CE, the beginning of the First Jewish Revolt against Rome, when many Jerusalem Christians fled the city for the safety of Pella (in modern Jordan). As you can observe at the model of 70 CE Jerusalem in the Israel Museum, during 41–43 CE the city walls were extended to include the western suburbs, but the revered tomb was not built over.

Probably to discourage Christian pilgrimage to and veneration of this holy spot, Hadrian filled in the quarry and built a Roman temple over it with a shrine to Aphrodite. But the Christian community never forgot what lay beneath, and in 325 CE at the Council of Nicea, the Bishop of Jerusalem, Macarius, asked Emperor Constantine to destroy the Roman temple and reveal to the world again the Tomb of Christ. Constantine then began building the first church on the spot in 326 CE, and it was finished in 335 CE. It included the area of the current church but was about twice the size. He had his engineers cut away the cliff behind the tomb-chamber so that it became a freestanding edifice centered in a circular rotunda. Sadly, the church was set on fire by the Persians in 614 CE but reconstructed by the Greek Orthodox patriarch of Jerusalem, Modestus. When Jerusalem came under

Muslim control in 638 CE, the church was protected for two ruling dynasties, the Umayyad and the Abbasid. But the mad Fatimid caliph Hakim destroyed it in 1009 CE, even hacking the Tomb of Christ with pickaxes (though eyewitness reports testify that the tomb-chamber was not completely destroyed). The current church was built in 1012–1170 CE.

History has granted governance of the Church of the Holy Sepulcher to six ancient Christian denominations. Their frequent quarrels resulted in giving the key to two Muslim families eight hundred years ago, in whose keeping it still remains in order to open the church every morning at dawn and lock it at dark. These six traditions are the Roman Catholics and five Eastern Orthodox: Greek, Coptic (Egyptian), Armenian, Syrian, and Ethiopic.

This is the holiest spot in Christendom, and the ardor of Christian pilgrims flocking to it can be overwhelming. I recommend you go to the church early in the morning before the crowds gather. There is nothing more sacred than entering this space in the quietude of the morning light. Once inside the door, the Stone of Unction will be before you—not ancient, but a traditional commemoration of the preparation of Jesus' body for burial and the focus of modern Orthodox Christian veneration. Watch and you will see anointing with oil, kissing, even the placing of babies upon it. In the East, the sense of holy space is much more vibrant than in the Western church. Certainly Protestants have to strain to appreciate (and they should) attachment to this place.

Take a sharp right upon entering the door to ascend what is left of Golgotha. Pilgrims and demolitions through the centuries have diminished it, but once you reach the top, you can see beneath the high Greek Orthodox altar the mount upon which Christ was crucified. A hole beneath the altar allows one, if desired, to touch it in veneration. To the right is the Roman Catholic altar illustrating the difference between the Eastern and Western churches: the Roman altar has its statue and the Greek its icon. The latter is troublesome to some Protestants, but it is instructive to bear in mind that the intent is not to portray merely the rabbi from Nazareth, but rather the God of the Nicene Creed.

Circle round to peer below, beyond the iconostasis of the Greek Orthodox chapel, and then descend a second set of stairs leading

Judea

down to the Stone of Unction. If you are with a group, it is important to gather the group here, because this is where pilgrims are lost or left behind. Proceed to the tomb by passing the beautiful but modern mosaic above the Stone of Unction and turn right to enter the tomb. Just opposite it is the spacious Greek Orthodox chapel. Inside the door of the chapel is a knee-high pillar with a circular button on top marking "the center of the universe" because it stands exactly halfway between Calvary and the tomb. The current shrine over the tomb, replacing a series of predecessors going back to the fourth century CE, dates only to 1810 CE.

How did this tomb get to be here and so close to Golgotha? The spot was a limestone quarry, in the middle of which was a flinty skull-shaped hill, good for nothing. So when the quarry was abandoned, the Romans appropriated the hill as an ideal place of crucifixion just outside the city gates. In the meantime, the quarry, as is often the case in this part of the world, had become a Jewish cemetery because of the ease of carving tombs into its soft limestone walls. This is what Joseph of Arimathea did, and enough of the burial bench remains to see where Jesus' shrouded body was laid. The inscription reads "He is not here! He is risen!" The tomb is managed by the Greek Orthodox Church, which dates back to the original church in the book of Acts.

The Coptic (Egyptian) Orthodox, also of a very ancient church, are relegated to the chapel behind the tomb, where they venerate what they believe to be a piece of the outside limestone wall. (Look beneath the altar to the oil lamp on the left.) Behind the Coptic chapel is the cave-chapel of the Syrian Orthodox Church, so ancient that their liturgy is in an Aramaic that the historical Jesus would have understood. It contains several unadorned first-century CE kokhim Jewish tombs, single chambered and simpler than Jesus', since his had been donated by a rich man. While today this is a very humble chapel, it is worth a visit on Sunday morning when it is adorned with carpets, wall hangings, flowers, icons, and a small welcoming community of three to thirty worshipers who celebrate the weekly Eucharist. Indeed, an excellent time to visit the Church of the Holy Sepulcher is early Sunday morning to witness the cacophony of Christian liturgies that emerged from that first Easter.

Exit to the left and make a sharp turn into the Roman Catholic

> **Renowned for its religious diversity, Jerusalem also demonstrates much of Christianity's cultural diversity.**

chapel to view the moving depiction of Abraham's sacrifice of Isaac (Genesis 22) in the rear area. Continue around to the left (restrooms are here) to the Armenian Chapel. If time allows, descend to the Crypt of St. Helena, noting the many ancient crosses carved by centuries of pilgrims. To the left of the central altar is a locked chamber, accessible only with permission from the Armenians, to more tombs, proving this was a cemetery. One of them bears graffiti with a ship, presumably the one upon which the pilgrim arrived. The stairs to the right of the altar lead down to a pit that is part of an Old Testament quarry, and where, as legend has it, Constantine's mother, Helena, discovered the original cross of Christ.

Come up and to the left again for a view of Golgotha below the place of the cross. A sharp turn left into the chapel reveals a crack in Golgotha, which tradition says was created by the earthquake at the time of Jesus' death. Continue left to exit the church.

Once outside, to appreciate further the cultural diversity of Christianity, turn left into the Coptic chapel and follow the hall around it to the left of the altar and up the stairs to the Ethiopic chapel, where a solitary monk is always on duty. If you ask him, he will probably chant for you from an ancient cross-shaped Ethiopic lectionary. (A small donation in the basket would be appreciated if you ask him to do this.) Note the African flavor of the large icon depicting the marriage of King Solomon to the queen of Sheba. Continue along the left-hand aisle of this chapel and out the exit door to the left of the altar, being careful not to bump your head on the low lintel.

You will now find yourself on the "roof," among the hovels where the Ethiopic monks live. In the center is the dome of the Crypt of St. Helena, which in the Middle Ages stood within an Augustinian monastery, built over the ruins of the basilica of Constantine's Church of the Holy Sepulcher.[42] Look round about you to see the vaulted ceilings of the monastery's refectory. Over them is the bell tower of the Lutheran Church of the Redeemer. At this point you

Judea

have two options. Continue farther to exit the "roof" through the open gate, which is the Ninth Station of the Cross on the Crusader Via Dolorosa; or retrace your steps back through the Ethiopic and Coptic chapels to the courtyard outside the Holy Sepulcher where the Church of the Redeemer is up the steps and to the left.

Church of the Redeemer

Lutheran Church of the Redeemer

Built over part of the same quarry that lies beneath the Church of the Holy Sepulcher, the Church of the Redeemer was built by German kaiser Wilhelm in 1898 CE. The excavations beneath the church can be visited by prior appointment (phone: 02-627-6111). Walking up the tower (open Monday–Saturday, 9 a.m.–1 p.m.; 1:30 p.m.–5 p.m.) is highly recommended for the view of the Holy Sepulcher and all of Jerusalem. The church is home to three congregations: German, Palestinian, and English-speaking. The latter, which gathers for Holy Eucharist at nine o'clock on Sunday mornings in the ancient Crusader Chapel adjacent to the main church, practices Eucharistic hospitality and functions as the Protestant Church in the Old City, where student-pilgrim groups of all denominations are welcome.

Bethesda Pools and St. Anne's Church

The Bethesda Pools (John 5:1-13) lay outside the city walls at the time of Jesus, near the "Sheep Gate." Today they are just inside the Lions'/St. Stephen's Gate of the Old City, up the hill from the Garden of Gethsemane and across the street from the northern end of the Temple Mount/Dome of the Rock mosque plaza. Like most churches in Jerusalem, St. Anne's Church is closed daily between noon and 2 p.m. and all day on Sundays. Restrooms are to the right, and the ticket counter is to the left. The excavations are forward,

Bethesda Pools

and beside them is the magnificent Crusader church built in 1138 CE. We do not know the names of Mary the mother of our Lord's parents, but the apocryphal Gospels seem to have supplied the name Hannah in Hebrew (Anne in English), based on the birth of Samuel in 1 Samuel 1. Nonetheless, this is a great place to sing praises and appreciate the magnificent acoustics (slower songs are better). *Ave Maria* is especially appropriate.

Via Dolorosa

Walking farther up the street into the Old City, you will meet the First and Second Stations of the Crusader Via Dolorosa, brought from medieval Europe and bearing no relation to history. But if you would like to walk it as a pious exercise, purchase the pamphlet for $1 at St. Anne's or on the street to guide you with prayer on your way. The Second Station of the Cross actually has two stops. The first contains two chapels and a helpful model of Jerusalem at the time of Jesus. The second part is the monastery of the French Sisters of Zion, under which, for a modest entrance fee, you can examine the archaeological excavations of Hadrian's Aelia Capotolina. This site was mistakenly thought by the Crusaders to be the floor of Antonia Fortress, which in fact did

"Fifth Station of the Cross"

sit above it but was not the praetorium of the Gospels. That was located between the current Zion and Jaffa Gates (see the section on the Armenian Quarter).

Judea

Snow on the Jewish tombs, Mount of Olives

⭐ Mount of Olives

Perched east of the Temple Mount and west of the Judean wilderness, this most famous of mountains is actually two hilltops easily recognizable by two towers: the Russian Orthodox monastery tower on the hillock to the south, and the stubby Lutheran tower of Augusta Victoria upon the hillock to the north. Further distinguishing the mount is the modernistic tower of the Hebrew University of Jerusalem, actually on Mount Scopus, a third hill just a bit farther to the north. So when approaching Jerusalem from Jericho or observing it from the Herodium, look for these three distinctive towers.

House with cave-barn in Bethany, similar to Jesus' in Bethlehem and Nazareth

Bethany

Bethany was Jesus' home away from home when he was in Jerusalem, because his buddies Lazarus, Mary, and Martha lived there. It is difficult to visit because of the current separation wall between Israel and the West Bank, which artificially cuts off a natural suburb of the city. It can be reached with effort, and the Tomb of Lazarus (John 11) has some claims to authenticity.

Saint Jerome records the existence of a church here in 390 CE. The original entrance was turned into a mosque because the

> Jesus' home away from home was Bethany.

Muslims venerated the raising of Lazarus, and at first they permitted Christians to visit. When this became increasingly difficult, the Franciscans cut the existing entrance to the tomb between 1566 and 1575 CE and built the current church and monastery in 1954 CE. In the church courtyard, the mosaic is of the fourth-century CE church and the pillars are of the fifth-century CE church. Restrooms are to the far right. The original entrance to the Tomb of Lazarus (visible inside) faces toward the mosque and church (east).

Franciscan chapel mural

Bethphage (House of the Unripe Fig)

This is where the Palm Sunday walk begins. It is the probable general location where Jesus' disciples procured the donkey (Mark 11:1-7). The fourth-century pilgrim Egeria mentions a church here, and in the middle of the current nineteenth-century CE church stands a square podium, from which the builders of a Crusader church pictured our Lord mounting the donkey. (They evidently had in mind European horses rather than Palestinian burros!) The beautiful paintings on the mounting stone are original. The wall murals are twentieth century CE.

> By riding a donkey on the Mount of Olives, Jesus was making a messianic statement.

Ezekiel prophesied that when the presence of God left the Temple, it took up residence on the Mount of Olives (11:23), where it will remain until it returns to the Temple from the Mount of Olives (43:2-5). Zechariah foresees that on the eschatological Day of the Lord, "he will stand upon" the two-hilled Mount of Olives, which will be "split in half" (14:4). By the time of Jesus, any Jew could tell you that when the Messiah manifests himself and the kingdom of God, it will be on the Mount of Olives. Likewise, Jesus knew very well what he was doing. By riding the animal over the Mount of Olives in fulfillment of the prophetic "Look, your king will come to you . . . humble and riding on an ass" (Zechariah 9:9), he was making a messianic statement. He also knew what it would elicit: adoration from the locals around Bethany and Bethphage, a perceived threat to the Jerusalem high priestly establishment, and an accusation of sedition by the Roman government.

Pater Noster (Our Father)

Moving down the Mount of Olives, you will reach the French convent Pater Noster, which is closed to visitors on Sundays (for Holy Mass). The cave at the center of the courtyard, in pre-Constantinian tradition, was where Jesus would seek refuge and teach his disciples, and it was also associated with his ascension. Eusebius reports that Constantine built three churches over three caves that were sites of the three chief mysteries of the faith: the stable in Bethlehem, the tomb cave near Golgotha, and the Ascension here. Helena, Constantine's mother, built the first church dedicated in 334 CE, the apse of which can be seen in the cave, with the title "Church of the Disciples and of the Ascension."

When the focus of the Ascension moved farther up the hill to the Mosque of the Ascension, the significance of this cave was increasingly associated with the teaching of Jesus, then specifically

ARAMEEN	HÉBREU
אבונה די בשמיא	אבינו אשר בשמים
יתקדש שמך	יתקדש שמך
תאתה מלכותך	תבוא מלכותך
תתעבד רעותך	יעשה רצונך
כדי בשמיא כן בארעא	כאשר בשמים ובארץ
לחמנו חב לנה סנוק יום ביומא	לחמנו תן לנו יום יומי
ושבק לנה חובינא	ושא לנו משאתנו
כדי אף אנחנה שבקנא לחיבינא	כאשר גם אנחנו נשאנו לחיבינו
ואל תעלנה לנסיון	ואל תביאנו במסה
אלא פצינה מן בישא	כי אם חיצנו מן הרשע
אמן	אמן

TEXTES ÉTABLIS   J. STARCKY — P. GRELOT
PAR LES RR.PP.   J. CARMIGNAC — E.PUECH
M.J. STÈVE

HOC FELIT A.MAISSERA ANNO MCMLXXXV

Lord's Prayer in Aramaic and Hebrew

with the giving of the Lord's Prayer. In 1102 CE, a pilgrim reported seeing a marble plaque with the Lord's Prayer; and in 1170 CE, another pilgrim likewise saw a Greek inscription beneath the altar. The sisters are trying to post the Lord's Prayer in every language of the world and are now approaching two hundred. Look for the language of your heritage. The Aramaic of Jesus is just outside the cave. English is up in the cloister.

From here you can walk down the hill to a broad staircase leading to the Mount of Olives. Turn right to descend the broad stairs, being careful of the steep and slippery pavement as well as the local automobile traffic.

Dominus Flevit (The Lord Wept)

This site commemorates two New Testament passages, Matthew 23:37-39 and Luke 19:41-44, that describe Jesus weeping over Jerusalem. That there was a Byzantine monastery here is evidenced by the mosaic-floored wine tank located outside at the far end of the property, overlooking the Kidron Valley. In front of the chapel itself is the lovely seventh-century CE mosaic floor depicting the "pearl of great price" being pierced and dividing a fish (the fish may be a symbol for the Last Supper). The modern chapel was built in 1955 CE by the Italian Antonio Barluzzi.[43] Its dome is shaped as a

Temple Mount from chapel window

teardrop surrounded by four vases, in which it was the custom to collect one's tears upon the death of a beloved.

Down by the wine tank, the view can be instructive. The Garden of Gethsemane is to your right, marked by the golden onion domes of the St. Mary Magdalene Russian Orthodox convent. To the south of the Temple Mount is the City of David. Behind the golden Dome of the Rock mosque is the double-domed Church of the Holy Sepulcher: the smaller black dome is over Golgotha, and the larger gray dome is over the Tomb of Christ.

Garden of Gethsemane and Church of All Nations

As you continue walking carefully down the busy street from Dominus Flevit, you will pass on your right the convent of St. Mary Magdalene. It is well worth a visit, but is open only on Tuesdays and Thursdays, 10 a.m. to noon. The garden where our Lord prayed and was arrested is farther down the street to the immediate left. Note that access to the rock where Jesus prayed closes at 11:45 a.m., opening again at 2:30 p.m.

It is almost impossible to kill an olive tree, and the root systems of these trees could go back two thousand years. This is assuredly the Garden of Gethsemane, which means "olive press." From

Gethsemane

Byzantine times or before, a certain broad rock was associated with Jesus' prayer of agony that the cup be taken from him. The drawings at the church's entrance depict the Byzantine and Crusader churches upon which this modern Church of All Nations is built. Around the rock is a crown of thorns with birds in a posture of submission, willing to drink from the chalice. It is a space to be quiet, and pictures are allowed except within the gate to the rock. You may enter to kneel upon this space hallowed by tradition with the permission of the Franciscan on duty.

> The root systems of these olive trees could go back two thousand years.

Modern "Mount Zion"

Byzantine Christians misunderstood the prophet Micah's synonymous parallelism (3:12). They took the Temple Mount (Har Har Ha-Bayit, "Mountain of the House" [of God]) and Zion to be two different hills in Jerusalem. Biblical Mount Zion is of course the Temple Mount, where the golden Dome of the Rock mosque stands today. But the Byzantine mistake was appropriated by the

Mount Zion

Crusaders, so the name of this western hill still appears on maps today as (pseudo-) "Mount Zion." It lay within the city walls of Jerusalem at the time of Jesus, and the sixth-century CE Madaba Map[44] proves it was within the Byzantine walls as well. Today it lies just outside the Zion Gate of the current sixteenth-century CE Old City walls.

Cenacle (Upper Room) and the "Tomb of David"

Both of these structures, which themselves are not ancient, sit above the foundation of a building dating back to Roman times, second century CE or earlier. Epiphanius of Salamis (315–403 CE) says the "little church of God" stood here in 130 CE. That church, because of heavy Roman persecution of Christianity, could not have been built in the second century CE and so must date to the first,

"Tomb of David"

probably to the origins of the Christian community in Jerusalem. The first house church of Jerusalem was "the upstairs room" of Acts 1:13, where the disciples gathered regularly with Mary, the mother of Jesus, after the Ascension; where they chose Matthias to replace Judas; and where we can assume they were gathered "all together in one place" on the day of Pentecost (Acts 2:1; attested by Cyril of Jerusalem, before 348 CE).

Acts 2:43-47 describes the life and growth of this nascent church that, this being the affluent part of Jerusalem at the time, evidently met in the house of a wealthy and generous early Christian, possibly even John Mark (Acts 12:12). It does not take much imagination to connect this upstairs room with the guest room, "a large room upstairs," where Mark says Jesus instituted the Lord's Supper (14:14-15). In the fourth century CE it was known as "the Upper Church of the Apostles," and in the fifth as "Zion, Mother of all the Churches," which is pictured prominently on the Madaba Map.

David was buried in the City of David (1 Kings 2:10), where archaeologists have discovered what was probably the royal necropolis (see the section on the City of David). But Byzantine piety enjoyed venerating both David, the Israelite founder of Jerusalem, and St. James, the founder of the Jerusalem church, at the Church of Zion. So traditions developed that David was buried here, and James just inside the modern Zion Gate at the Armenian cathedral (same hill; the current wall is an artificial divide).

You may reach the Cenacle/David's Tomb by exiting Zion Gate or driving to the parking lot outside it. Walk toward the imposing Dormition Abby, taking the left path at the Y. Walk straight through the passageway, then keep to the left until you reach the courtyard of the fourteenth-century CE Franciscan monastery to enter "the Tomb of David." The cenotaph (a monument to honor a person whose remains are elsewhere) is Crusader, but the niche behind it was probably a receptacle in the apse of the Byzantine Church of Mount Zion.

Exit the passageway through which you entered to get back to the street, and turn right through a doorway to enter the Cenacle. While remnants may be Crusader, the present reconstruction is fourteenth-century CE Gothic from the Franciscan monastery built in 1335 CE. Most interesting is the pillar in the corner with the

Christian symbol of a mother pelican who willingly sacrifices the flesh of her breast for her hungry chicks. Suleiman the Magnificent of the Ottoman Turks dispelled the Christians and turned the room into a mosque venerating "the Prophet David." The *mihrab* (semi-circular niche in the mosque's wall) facing the direction of Mecca and the Arabic prohibiting public prayer are witnesses to this. The spot came under Israeli control in 1948 and is now open to all. (The Cenacle closes at 1 p.m. on Fridays.)

Church of the Dormition

Church of the Dormition

The Church of the Dormition is German, built over the Crusader church to St. Mary in 1900 by Kaiser Wilhelm. From the beginning of Christianity, as we see in Acts 1:13-14, the disciples gathered around Mary, the mother of our Lord, who stood at the foot of the cross and was proclaimed by the early church as *Theotokos*, mother of God. The Greek Orthodox Church, the oldest church in the world, has always venerated Mary; and Martin Luther's Marian devotion would astonish modern Protestants. The God of the Bible has a history of receiving into heaven the bodies of special individuals (Enoch, Elijah, Moses). Many traditions include Mary in this group, citing the Dormition of the Virgin, when, according to tradition, she fell asleep and was taken into heaven.

Saint Peter in Gallicantu

Saint Peter in Gallicantu (St. Peter at the Cock's Crow) is a lovely French Catholic church, beautifully restored in 1997. It is a great place to read the Gospel narrative of Jesus' trial before the high priest Annas/Caiaphas (Mark 14:53-65) and to view the model of Byzantine Jerusalem. However, the trial probably did not

Saint Peter in Gallicantu

take place here. The earliest church at this place is from the fifth or sixth century CE, and the "prison" over which it lies was actually a barn. (The stone loops that tour guides like to tell you were used to bind prisoners were actually used to tether animals, as is known from similar sites.) A better contender for the high priest's house would be at the top of the hill near the Church of the Dormition, where Herodian upper-class homes have been uncovered on the Armenian property; or up in the current Jewish Quarter among the high priestly family mansions excavated there (see the section on the Jewish Quarter of the Old City). However, as a devotional spot, Saint Peter in Gallicantu is worth a visit, and the view from the rear overlook of the City of David, of the Kidron, Hinnom, and Tyropoean Valleys, the Mount of Olives, and the Temple Mount, is worth the minimal entrance fee.

Valley Tombs to Explore (Kidron and Hinnom)

In the Kidron Valley, between the Temple Mount and the Garden of Gethsemane, there are three striking Jewish catacomb tombs cut into the rock cliff, to which all kinds of legendary associations have been attached. The one in the middle we can identify by its Hebrew inscription as the (second-century BCE) tomb of the priestly family of Hezir (1 Chronicles 24:15; Nehemiah 10:20). The

Kidron Valley tombs

other two date to the first century BCE: the one to the left/north bears the popular name "Absalom's Pillar" (2 Samuel 18:18); and the one to the right/south with the pyramid on top is the "Tomb of Zachariah."

At the southern end of the Kidron, En Rogel, the valley turns west and becomes the Hinnom Valley (*Ge Hinnom* in Hebrew; *Gehenna* in Greek). In and around the monastery of Aceldama was a large Jewish cemetery, of the New Testament period and earlier, that includes tombs from wealthy and prominent families, the most interesting of which is the tomb of Annas, the high priest and father-in-law of Caiaphas.

Yad Vashem

The Holocaust museum and memorial is open Sunday–Thursday, 9 a.m.–5 p.m.; until 8 p.m. on Thursdays; and until 2 p.m. on Fridays and holiday eves; closed on Shabbat and all Jewish holidays. Entrance is free, but reservations are required for groups. Headset-recorded tours may be rented. For contact information, go to www.yadvashem.org. The name comes from Isaiah 56:5, which is inscribed opposite the Hall of Remembrance: "I will give them, in My House and within My walls, a monument and a name [*yad vashem*] . . . which shall not perish" (JPS Tanakh).

Young Israelis at ghetto uprising memorial

If you have a reservation, arrive early at the reception hall. Restrooms and a coffee shop are located downstairs, as well as lockers. You may not bring bags or backpacks into the museum. It is a solemn and reverent place, so no photography is allowed inside the buildings. Cell phones must also be turned off, there is no gum chewing, and a quiet demeanor must be kept throughout the premises. Just outside the reception hall to the right is an excellent book and gift shop.

You can spend as long as your time will allow at the museum, but allow one hour minimum. As you enter, note the movie of the vibrant life of the Jewish community in Europe before Hitler's atrocity began. At the end of the zigzag path of the museum is a room on the left to sit for some quiet meditation. Turn left out the exit to a plaza, with restrooms and a coffee shop, from which you can ascend the stairs/escalator to the Hall of Remembrance. Here an eternal flame burns amid a map of the Nazi concentration camps. Per the Jewish custom of respect, men wear a head covering.

Exiting the hall, turn left around the building to approach the tall memorial meant to recall the smokestacks of the crematoria. It is inscribed with a Kaddish, the Jewish memorial prayer for the dead. Continue up the path to the Children's Memorial, which is the most moving one for many. Among the six million Jews who perished in the Holocaust, 1.5 million were children. A father and a mother who lost their son wanted to build a memorial, but how? They decided on the principle of "the one for the many." The name and face of their beautiful boy is inscribed at the entrance. Inside, a single central lamp produces 1.5 million lights, and the names of the lost children are recited twenty-four hours a day, with their birthdays, in Hebrew, German, and English. Just before you enter this building, note the artwork outside to the left: narrow limestone pillars broken at the top, representing lives cut short.

Take a sharp right outside the Children's Memorial and follow the path past Janusz Korczak Square, which commemorates Janusz Korczak for saving many Jewish orphans. Walking farther brings you to the entrance hall where you began, but before returning to it, note to the right the "Avenue of Righteous Gentiles," lined with carob trees, each one planted in memory of a non-Jew who saved Jews. Schindler's tree is one of the first ones on the right side of the path. At the end of the pathway are two artistic renditions. The one on the right shows ghetto Jews being forced into the concentration camps by the Nazis and beneath it the Hebrew words "Out of your murders comes life." To the left, a statuary of the Holocaust ghetto uprisings ascends to modern Israeli soldiers, men and women, who say to the world, "Never Again!"

Chagall Windows

Inspired especially by the blessings of Jacob and Moses on the tribes of Israel (Genesis 49 and Deuteronomy 33), Marc Chagall called these twelve magnificent windows his "gift to the Jewish people." Enter Hadassah Hospital En Kerem by the beautiful main entrance, walk forward, and take the hall that veers to the right. The synagogue will be at the end of the hall on the right, and payment for entrance is on the left.

Tribe of Levi

Open Sunday–Thursday, 8:00 a.m.–12:30 p.m. and 2:00 p.m.–3:30 p.m.; 10 shekels per person; group rates are available. A docent will give you a brief introduction to the synagogue and then will play an informative recording explaining the windows. Reservations are not necessary (phone: 02-677-6271).

Temple Mount

Israel Museum

Open Sunday, Monday, Wednesday, and Thursday, 10 a.m.–5 p.m.; Tuesday, 4 p.m.–9 p.m.; Friday and holiday eves, 10 a.m.–2 p.m.; Shabbat and holidays, 10 a.m.–5 p.m.. For details and special exhibitions, visit www.english.imjnet.org.il. Entrance for groups is to the right of the main entrance (just in front of the model of Herodian Jerusalem). If you are not in a group, go in the main entrance, turn right past the Shrine of the Book, and go down to the scale model (50:1) of the Temple.

It is best to begin facing the front of the Temple. You can see the spheres of holiness, the Court of the Gentiles, narrowing into the Court of the Women and leading to the Court of the Priests, where the altar is and where worship took place. Only the priests entered the Temple building, and only the high priest entered the holy of holies one day a year, on Yom Kippur, the Day of Atonement. Gaze to the left, and you will see Herod's apartments above the col-umned Royal Portico, with Solomon's Portico in front of you on the corner overlooking the valley (John 10:23). Turn your sight to the right, and you will see the massive four-towered Antonio Fortress where the Roman garrison was stationed to preclude any messianic uprising, which surely would arise from the Temple Mount. Turn your gaze farther to your right, and you will see the Bethesda Pools, which were outside the city walls at the time of Jesus.

Move left and you will be overlooking the Old Testament City of David, which in the time period of the model was a wealthy district that included the palace of Queen Helena of Adiabene, an Iraqi convert to Judaism. The Gihon Spring is in the Kidron Valley below the ancient City of David area, and as you continue walking left and around, you will see the Siloam Pool. A bit farther, there is a red arrow on the outer wall of the Temple Mount pointing out the current Jewish Western Wall. Still farther to the left and up is the upper-class neighborhood where Jesus was tried by Caiaphas/Annas. The Last Supper and Pentecost probably took place here.

Go around to stand at the rear of the Temple Mount. On the western side, outside a gate, is a bowl-shaped depression that represents the limestone rock quarry, in the middle of which is a skull-shaped flinty hill, Golgotha. Here Jesus was crucified, just outside the Garden Gate, in a quarry that had become a garden cemetery. If you look closely, in the left lip of the bowl is a rock-cut tomb. (See the sections on the Armenian Quarter of the Old City and the Holy Sepulcher Church.)

Walk up the stairs above the model and enter the courtyard of the Shrine of the Book, Israel's museum memorial to the Dead Sea Scrolls. You will see a white dome sprayed with water, symbolic of the lids of the jars in which the scrolls were found, and of the daily baptisms of the Jewish Essene community at Qumran. On the other side is a black monolith representing the Sons of Light and the Sons of Darkness, apocalyptic foes in the scrolls. Descend beneath the black monolith to enter the jar of the white lid. In the antechamber, beginning on the right side, is a pictorial history of the scrolls' discovery. Sometimes there are special exhibitions in this area.

Continue through the tunnel to enter the main museum, which has two floors. The upper floor shows you examples of the Dead Sea Scrolls manuscripts, translations of the Bible (the scroll in the center circular pavilion

Golgotha, where Jesus was crucified, is a skull-shaped flinty hill.

is a copy of the Isaiah Scroll), books of exegesis, rules of the community, and other documents. Downstairs the Aleppo Codex, the oldest copy of the Hebrew Bible/Old Testament in book form, is displayed with commentary. Exit the Shrine of the Book, not where you entered but through the opposite door. To the right are restrooms. Exit the long exterior hallway, turn right, and ascend the steep hill to the Archaeological Wing.

Archaeological Wing of the Israel Museum

Holy of holies, Solomon's Temple, Arad

Proceed from the main entrance forward until you see a large apple on your left. Enter the building forward of the apple. There will be a restaurant and restrooms on your left and a gift shop on your right. Immediately past the restrooms, turn left into the biblical archaeology section of the building, which is divided into eras numbered 1–6. After exploring the different eras, leave the Israel Museum through the main exit straight down the central promenade. Just outside to the left is a great bookstore and gift shop.

Lodged at the entrance to the parking lot of the Israel Museum is the Bible Lands Museum Jerusalem, designed especially for students. Their website (www.blmj.org/en/) describes the museum's mission as follows: "The BLMJ's core exhibition invites you to explore the peoples, cultures and civilizations of the region of the Bible lands. As you walk through the galleries you'll travel thousands of years back in time, to the days when our nomadic forefathers first put down roots in settled communities. You'll witness the drama of civilization on the rise—from the beginning of writing, to the establishment of religions, to the birth of technologies for art, agriculture and war." Special exhibitions are also offered.

Judea

Jaffa Gate

Free Day in Jerusalem: Places to Explore

Orientation

The Jerusalem Tourist Information Center is just inside Jaffa Gate to the left (open Saturday–Thursday, 8:30 a.m.–5:00 p.m.; Friday 8:30 a.m.–1:30 p.m.). The Christian Information Center is just inside Jaffa Gate to the right (open Monday–Friday, 8:30 a.m.–5:30 p.m.; Saturday, 8:30 a.m.–12:30 p.m.). These places will provide you with more information about all the options listed here, as well as other sites and activities for a free day spent in Jerusalem.

Tower of David Museum of the History of Jerusalem

This museum is located just inside the Jaffa Gate to the right (open Sunday–Thursday, 10 a.m.–5 p.m.; Shabbat, 10 a.m.– 4 p.m.; open Fridays during July and August, 10 a.m.–2 p.m.).

Tower of David Museum of the History of Jerusalem

Judea

Damascus Gate

Ramparts Walk

Walk around the Old City atop its sixteenth-century CE walls. You must be in good physical shape, as there are a lot of ups and downs. Tickets are available just outside (southwest side) the Jaffa Gate beneath the minaret. Your ticket allows you to walk both ways. The Southern Ramparts are from Jaffa Gate to Dung Gate; the Northern Ramparts are from Jaffa Gate to Lions' Gate. (You can also purchase a ticket for the Northern Ramparts only at Damascus Gate.) Winter hours: Sunday–Thursday and Shabbat, 9 a.m.–4 p.m.; Friday, 9 a.m.–2 p.m. Summer hours: Sunday–Thursday and Shabbat, 9 a.m.–5 p.m.; Friday, 9 a.m.–2 p.m. During July and August, the Southern Ramparts are also open 7 a.m.–10 p.m. The Northern Ramparts are closed on Fridays year-round.

Roman Plaza at Damascus Gate

As you are facing the gate from outside the Old City, walk right and then left down the stairs. This is also where you can enter to walk the ramparts for the northern section only (for a fee of eight shekels). Here is the plaza built by Hadrian in 135 CE when he transformed Jerusalem into Aelia Capitolina, a Roman polis that by definition required a *cardo* running north to south through the center

Roman Plaza at Damascus Gate

of the city. In the middle of the plaza, he placed a statue of himself on top of a tall victory column, which is immortalized in the Arabic name of the gate, Bab el-Amud (Gate of the Pillar). This pillar is pictured in the oldest extant map of the Holy Land, the Madaba Map (sixth century CE), a replica of which rests within the current plaza, as well as within the excavated (Byzantine) *cardo* in the Jewish Quarter.

The gate, with an adjacent tower (to its left), was first built by Herod Agrippa I (41–44 CE) as part of his expansion of the walls of Jerusalem.[45] Hadrian remodeled the gate to become the ornamental entrance to his Roman city: a large central arch with two smaller pedestrian gates on either side. What you are seeing is merely the pedestrian gate to the left of the large central gate, which now lies beneath the Damascus Gate. Byzantine Christians called it St. Stephen's Gate, after the first martyr of the church, and connected it with the narrative in Acts 7:54-60. The remains of St. Stephen's Church are just outside the gate and up Nablus Road (at École Biblique).

> **St. Stephen's Gate is named for Christianity's first martyr.**

Rockefeller Archaeological Museum

Rockefeller Archaeological Museum

Located in East Jerusalem, just outside the Herod Gate of the Old City, the Rockefeller provides an intimate atmosphere with a crisp and clean chronological presentation of its artifacts to students of the history and archaeology of the Holy Land. For special exhibitions, see www.english.imjnet.org.il/page_1684. Please note that opening times for this museum are limited: Sunday, Monday, Wednesday, Thursday, 10 a.m.–3 p.m.; Saturday, 10 a.m.–2 p.m.; closed on Tuesday, Friday, and holiday eves.

Emmaus

The location of Emmaus (Luke 24) is a conundrum. The ancient Gospel manuscripts differ on whether it was 60 stadia (ca. 7 miles) or 160 stadia (ca. 19 miles). The former would be Abu Gosh, with its magnificent Crusader church. The latter would be Latrun, with its Byzantine church ruins. Abu Gosh is in fact the Old Testament Kiriath-jearim, where the ark of the covenant rested for twenty years (1 Samuel 6:21–7:2; see the section on Bet Shemesh). It is also a great place for a closing Mass to conclude your pilgrimage (previous reservation and permission required). Eucharist can also be celebrated outdoors within the ruins of the Byzantine church at Emmaus-Nicopolis (adjacent to the monastery of Latrun). The most likely location of Emmaus is the ancient synagogue with first-century CE ruins located to

> There is confusion about the exact location of Emmaus.

Judea

Roman road west of Jerusalem

the right of modern Highway 1, just as you exit Jerusalem at the right-angle turn below Motza (a gray stone building just outside the "Welcome to Jerusalem" sign). This site is a Sabbath day's journey from Jerusalem, sixty stadia round-trip.

⭐ Bethlehem

> As for you, Bethlehem of Ephrathah,
> 	though you are the least significant of Judah's forces,
> 		one who is to be a ruler in Israel on my behalf
> 			will come out from you.
> His origin is from remote times,
> 	from ancient days. (Micah 5:2)

David was born in Bethlehem, and contrary to the failed Saul, the warrior who was described as standing head and shoulders above all the others, David the shepherd was the runt of the litter. Likewise, the prophet Micah anticipated the Messiah to come not from the citadel of mighty Jerusalem, where most would expect, but from the lowly village of Bethlehem, lying just to the south.

David was from the tribe of Judah, the clan of Ephrathah, and the town of Bethlehem. As the first Roman emperor, Caesar

Judea

Church of the Nativity

Augustus initiated the *Pax Romana* and hence ordered a census of his empire. As was the case with David's census of his kingdom (2 Samuel 24; 1 Chronicles 21), Augustus's census probably had two motives: vanity to see how many people he ruled, and the money to be gained by so many taxes. There is evidence that Quirinius (Luke 2:2) began his service to Augustus in Syria about 9 BCE. The population census was a slow process implemented in two stages: first, property had to be registered; and only later in the second stage was the tax actually collected. It is this second stage that caused the uprising of Judas the Galilean in 6 CE, reported by Josephus[46] and referred to in Acts 5:37. Luke's account of the engaged couple's journey from Nazareth to Bethlehem regards the first stage of the census, the registration of property.

Since we know that Herod the Great was alive when Jesus was born, and that he died in 4 BCE, Jesus must have been born between 9 and 4 BCE. (Our current calendar originated with the monk Dionysius Exiguus [died ca. 550 CE], whose calculations were off by a few years.) Joseph was also from Bethlehem, and Jesus was probably born at Joseph's family's house. It would have been typical of the rural Palestinian village: two rooms built of stone adjacent to a cave used as the barn. Luke recounts that when it came time for Mary to give birth, she went to the cave-barn because there was no place for them in the *kataluma*, the "guest room" (Luke 2:7).[47] This is the same word used for the room that Jesus and his disciples, being pilgrims from out of town, used in Jerusalem for the Passover (Mark 14:14; Luke 22:11). What was probably the home of Joseph's parents was occupied with day-to-day activities and perhaps other guests, and Mary needed her privacy, which the stable provided.

Already in the second century CE, Justin Martyr and the

Protoevangelium of James (an apocryphal Gospel probably written about 145 CE) speak of the cave in which Jesus was born, and in the third century CE, Origen and Eusebius mention it as well. At the conclusion of the Second Jewish Revolt in 135 CE, Hadrian's Roman rule converted the cave into a pagan fertility shrine of Tammuz-Adonis. Why would Rome do this unless the cave had become, apparently already in the first century, a place of veneration by Christian Jews? Ironically, this action marked the spot for posterity, and in 395 CE Jerome celebrated the cave's return to Christian custody.[48]

Queen Helena (Constantine's mother) dedicated the first church over the cave-stable in 339 CE, the mosaic floor of which is visible beneath the floor in the center of today's church—which, apart from the roof and floor, is the same as when Roman emperor Justinian built it in 529 CE. The Persian invasion of 614 CE spared it because the magi in the mosaic on the facade appeared Persian, making this the oldest church in the Holy Land. The first Crusader kings were crowned here. The Mamluks and the Ottoman Turks abused the building, allowing in animals, carts, and looting, which explains the tiny door through which you now enter. The highest lintel was the original entrance, and there were two more just like it on either side, now obscured by later building additions. The lower arch is Crusader.

Upon entering, note the cruciform baptismal font to the right and the mosaic floors of Helena in the center. The Crusaders added the paintings on the pillars and the mosaics above them. The church is in the basilica style, popular during the Byzantine period, with the high Greek Orthodox altar over the cave. Syrian and Armenian altars are to the left. Descent into the cave is from the right. Centuries of pious veneration have focused on the silver star as the place of the birth, and many pilgrims are moved to kneel before the mystery of the Incarnation. On the other side of the cave, now sunken, contemplation focuses on "she laid him in a manger" (Luke 2:7).

Exit the door opposite the one through which you entered the cave, and up the stairs bear right into the Roman Catholic Church of St. Catherine to experience the difference between the Eastern and Western churches. Saint Jerome translated the Bible into Latin (the Vulgate) in Bethlehem, and a set of stairs in the rear of the church descend to a cave identified as his cell, near a raised slab marked as his tomb, neither of which has historical foundation.

Judea

> The walls are painted bright colors in the tradition of Byzantine churches. Note the changing expression of the dog.

The miracle of the shepherds took place in the Judean hill country of Bethlehem. One place for the pilgrim to contemplate this is the Roman Catholic site in Beit Sahour, with its lovely Barluzzi chapel,[49] shepherds' caves, and outdoor altars, all of which can be reserved for a service or visited informally as available for the reading of scripture and singing of hymns.[50]

Luke reports that Zechariah and Elizabeth, both from priestly families, lived in the Judean hill country, and since Zechariah served at the temple in Jerusalem, their home was likely not too far from Bethlehem. Mary, engaged to Joseph from Bethlehem, was a relative of Elizabeth, whom she visited during her pregnancy (Luke 1:39-40). We can only speculate that Joseph and Mary might have met in the hill country, or perhaps in Nazareth where the groom may have been already seeking work as a builder in nearby Zippori (see the section on Zippori). Tradition, without historical foundation, located the family of John the Baptist in En Kerem, now in south Jerusalem. If time allows, a visit to the two churches there is worthwhile, if only to absorb the beauty and ambiance of the hill country. (The excursion could be combined profitably with your visit to the Chagall windows at Hadasa Hospital.)

The magi who sought to visit Jesus, as recounted by Matthew, were Persian-Babylonian astronomers and sages, probably of the priestly and/or ruling class. Tacitus and Suetonius attest that there was widespread expectation at the time that the ruler of the world would come from Judah, speculation that Josephus in fact related to Vespasian.[51] Babylon was the nucleus of scientific astronomy at the time, as cuneiform tablets with planetary calculations confirm. It is well established that in 7–6 BCE, the conjunction of Jupiter and Saturn in the constellation of Pisces created an unusually bright luminary. For ancient astronomers, Jupiter represented the Babylonian god Marduk, and Saturn represented the Jewish people. Their conjunction led the magi, who as sages had doubtless also scrutinized the Hebrew scriptures, to Herod in Jerusalem, whose paranoia is well documented. For instance, Herod executed his sons Alexander, Aristobulus, and Antipater because he perceived them as threats to his kingship. He also killed a host of Pharisees, along with their sympathizers, who prophesied that his "throne would be taken from him, both from himself and his descendants."[52]

Thus, for good reason, Joseph decided to take his family to Egypt, the traditional place of refuge for Judeans (1 Kings 11:40; 2 Kings 25:26; Jeremiah 26:21). Upon return, since Herod's rule had passed to his son Archelaus, whose disposition matched his father's, Joseph and Mary made their home in the village of Nazareth. From there, Joseph could obtain work as a builder in the city of Sepphoris (see the sections on Nazareth and Zippori).

Moving a mountain

Herodium (National Park)

Also known as: Herodion

Lying between Bethlehem and the Dead Sea, on the cusp of the Judean hill country and the Judean wilderness, sits King Herod's fortress-palace built between 23 and 20 BCE. Originally there were two mountains at the site. One was leveled to reinforce the other for the Herodium. One can imagine Jesus' disciples standing on the Mount of Olives, from where the Herodium is visible, and recalling

Judea

their Lord saying that if they had faith only the size of a mustard seed, they could move mountains (Matthew 17:20). If the scoundrel Herod could, why not the power of God?

Pass through the entrance gate up the hill and view, on the way up, the lower palace, notable by its pillared swimming pool with an island in the middle. Also note around the landscape humble Palestinian homes built next to barns, recalling the narrative of Bethlehem. The elongated flat, narrow oval, which extends from the pool-palace garden complex toward Herod's tomb to the right, is part of the funeral path. Described by Josephus, it was built when Herod's body was brought from Jericho, where he died, to be buried here at the Herodium.

Just before the top of the tel is a sign directing you to a sharp turn left to Herod's tomb, facing Jerusalem upon a promenade leading up the mountain. There is also a theater. At the apex of the tel, pause to absorb the geography. To the west, you can see Bethlehem and the Judean hill country; to the east, the Dead Sea and the Judean wilderness. To the north is Jerusalem, recognizable by the three towers on the Mount of Olives. Gazing below into the tel, you can see Herod's fortress-palace defended by four towers: the one on the left (southeast) is round, and the other three are semicircular. The baths were immediately below you to the right. Just beyond that was the triclinium (dining room) of Herod, which the Zealots turned into a synagogue.

Walk around the top of the tel to your right toward the northwest (Jerusalem/Bethlehem), and gaze southward down the Judean mountains. South of Bethlehem (which can be distinguished by the white steeple on the horizon that looks like an upside-down ice-cream cone) is the Arab village of Tekoa, from which the prophet Amos hailed. Farther to the south, along the mountain ridge but out of sight, sits Hebron. Descend into the excavated tel by means of the broad stairs.

Upon Herod's death in 4 BCE, the Herodium was inherited by his son Archelaus, who ruled only ten years. Then the palace became, like the formerly Herodian praetoria of Caesarea and Jerusalem, the property of the Roman procurators. But in 68 CE, during the First Jewish Revolt, the Zealots captured the Herodium from the Romans and made it their fortress-hideaway, until the Roman army defeated them in 70 CE. The site sat vacant until the Second Jewish Revolt, when the Jewish rebels once again made this their desert headquarters from 132 to 135 CE. With Rome's second and decisive victory, the hill lay in ruins and was abandoned until, like Masada farther south, Byzantine monks took up residence here in the fifth through seventh centuries CE.

The rectangular open area of the excavations was the Herodian courtyard. Into its side, beneath the sole circular tower, the Zealots installed a mikveh, or religious ritual bath. Just opposite the mikveh is a set of stairs descending to the cisterns, some of which the Zealots connected with a tunnel system, enabling them to sneak in and out without the notice of the Romans. Walk down the stairs, being careful not to bump your head on the low door, and pause. Look up to see a hole where, during the Herodian period, servants would drop the water bucket on a rope into the cistern from above. Follow the tunnels to the "main cistern," where you can see at ground level a door opening out to what would have been the cistern's original entrance and stairs. Leave the main cistern and continue into the final corridor, where, against the wall, is a map explaining the system of cisterns and tunnels used by the Zealots. Exit to the outside at the side of the tel, turn left, and take the upper path to return to the parking lot.

Judea

Monastery of St. George in Wadi Kelt

One of the oldest monasteries of the Byzantine desert monks in the Holy Land and the world was built during the fifth and sixth centuries CE. It was built around a cave that Greek Orthodox tradition associates with Elijah's cave of Horeb (1 Kings 19), and with the place where an angel revealed to Joachim that his wife, Anne, would bear the Virgin Mary. The central church of the monastery is dedicated to the Virgin, through whose intercession the monks believe miracles have occurred. In a glass coffin is Saint John (1913–1960 CE), who lived alone at the monastery and whose body has not deteriorated. The monastery is named for Saint George of Koziba, who lived here during the sixth century CE. The

> The monastery is built around a cave that is associated with Elijah.

Monastery of St. George

monks here identify with the hermit ascetic John the Baptist, who was active near here. Sadly, the monastery was destroyed by the Persian invasion in 614 CE, and many monks were killed. But it was rebuilt and continues to offer hospitality to pilgrims to this day.

From the highway connecting Jerusalem and Jericho, exit left at the sign to Wadi Kelt. Follow the winding road to the upper entrance and take the broad cement path down to the monastery. Inside, coffee, juice, and cookies are provided, as well as restrooms. The church is on the main floor, and the cave is upstairs. Exit the monastery down just a bit to take a sharp left for the trail to Jericho. This is a magnificent path along the wadi (valley) that takes about two hours. Beneath the modern aqueduct on the opposite side, you can occasionally see Herod's original aqueduct, which brought springwater to his winter palace at Jericho, which is where the trail ends. A brief tour of the palace can be enjoyed if time allows. You should have transportation waiting for you at the spot where you climb out of the wadi to transfer you to Jericho for lunch. The monastery is open every day, 9 a.m.–1 p.m.; start early.

Jericho

At thirteen hundred feet below sea level, Jericho is the lowest and, with city walls and tower built ten thousand years ago,

Oldest structure on earth

the oldest, city on earth. The primary excavations at Tel al-Sultan were conducted by Kathleen Kenyon between 1952 and 1958 as she developed the emerging archaeological method of stratigraphy, that is, dating by layers of civilization (she found twenty-three!). The top of the tel (under the canopy where there is seating) provides an excellent view of Mount Nebo to the east, from which God showed Moses the Promised Land. To the northwest is the traditional "Mount of Temptation," where twelfth-century CE Crusaders located Jesus' temptation by Satan to view and receive all the nations of the world. In 1895, the Greek Orthodox Church built a monastery there, which can be reached by foot or by using the gondola at the base of the tel. To the south is "Elisha's Spring" (2 Kings 2:19-22), which accounts for the existence of the ancient oasis and the lush vegetation you see before you. (It can be visited by crossing the street at the base of the tel on the gondola side.) Between Mount Nebo and where you are standing, Joshua brought the Israelites into the Promised Land, and Jericho was the first Canaanite city they encountered.

Walk from the covered overlook toward the "Mount of Temptation" to see below you the (defensive?) tower, which is the oldest human structure in the world to date (Stone Age, ca. 8000 BCE). It includes an interior stairway with twenty steps. Husbandry (the domestication of plants and animals) began here at Jericho, and also the production of pottery. Neolithic artwork, tools, and weapons testify to the

> **In Jericho is the oldest human structure in the world, dating to the Stone Age, ca. 8000 BCE.**

Judea

sophistication of the oldest city's residents. They were also spiritual, as witnessed by an evident "Cult of the Skulls" (which were separated from the bodies and plastered), and by the burial of bodies beside the entrance to domestic dwellings. Cast your eyes just above the tower into the excavated tel to the right and the left, and you will see remnants of mud brick wall from the Bronze Age city (ca. 2000 BCE). If time allows, visitors can explore the site and read the many diagrammed signs describing the finds. Curiously, no walls have been found dating to the time of Joshua's entry, ca. 1200 BCE. Perhaps the town Joshua met was poorly walled. The Hebrew says simply, "The wall collapsed" (Joshua 6:20).

"New Testament Jericho" lies to the west of the tel and the modern city. It can be explored at the end of your hike of Wadi Kelt, or by walking down from the Wadi Kelt road. Most impressive is Herod the Great's winter palace, built with gardens on both sides of the wadi. As you enter from the west (the Jerusalem side), you will meet the main reception hall, then a royal court, the bathhouse facing another royal court, a T-shaped reception hall, and then an adjacent wing at a lower level. In front of the main reception hall and first royal court is the front portico, facing a mirror image of itself on the opposite side of the wadi (south). Herod drowned his son Antipater, as well as his brother-in-law, Aristobulus, in the palace's swimming pools. Five days later, he died here at Jericho, and his body was taken in grand procession for burial at his desert palace between Bethlehem and the Judean wilderness, the Herodium.[53]

If you have extra time, there are two other sites of note. A Byzantine synagogue boasts a fifth–sixth century CE mosaic including the Hebrew inscription *Shalom al Yisrael*, "Peace be upon Israel." There is also Hisham's Palace, which was built by one of the early Muslim rulers of the Holy Land (the Arab Umayyad dynasty). As you enter, note the beautiful six-pointed star, which was probably a window decoration. You will be in the courtyard with the residence and small mosque round about. To the right is the bathhouse, north of which is the most beautiful mosaic in the country: the Tree of Life. Its fifteen fruits represent the countries under the rule of the Umayyad dynasty. The gazelles to the left are allies, and the one being attacked by a lion on the right is an enemy.

Crossing into the country of Jordan is possible nearby at the

Allenby Bridge. Crossing is also available in Galilee at the King Hussein Bridge, or in the far south on the Red Sea at Eilat/Aqaba.

Byzantine "across the Jordan in Bethany"

Qaser El Yahud (Baptismal Site)

The scripture "across the Jordan in Bethany" (John 1:28) refers to the wilderness north of the Sea of Galilee (Batenea); see the section on Bethsaida. Plans are under consideration to make that site on the Jordan River more easily accessible. The river can also be accessed just south of Tiberias at Yardenit, a site operated by a Jewish kibbutz. The Byzantine church is located "across the Jordan in Bethany," on the current Jordanian side of the river just across from Qaser El Yahud, which is on the Israeli side near Jericho. That John the Baptist conducted part of his ministry in this area is clear from Matthew 3:1: "In those days John the Baptist appeared in the desert of Judea." It is an appropriate spot for an Affirmation of Baptism service, if your group so desires. Parking and restrooms are available.

Qumran (National Park)

The origins and occupants of Qumran are shrouded in mystery, so a bit of history might shed some light. When the Jews returned

Judea

from Babylon to Judah after the exile, they rebuilt the Temple (520–515 BCE), and it is evident from the books of Haggai and Zechariah that they intended to reestablish the monarchy. However, since they were only the province of Yehud within the Persian Empire, their overlords would not allow this. So what developed instead was a hierocracy, a government ruled over by the high priest.

During the Hellenistic period, under the rule of the Seleucid (Syrian) dynasty, the high priesthood became increasingly politicized. After the successful Maccabean Revolt (164 BCE), the Jewish family of the Hasmoneans became the rulers of Judah, and the politicization of the temple administration continued. During the Jewish war for independence of 167–164 BCE, the supporters of the Maccabees, the Hasidim, were divided over the issue of whether it was permissible to defend themselves when attacked on the Sabbath. The more "liberal" group, which allowed for fighting on the Sabbath in extreme circumstances, emerged as part of a sect known as the Pharisees—who believed the world is basically good and sought to help faithful Jews live in it according to God's laws (the Torah). The more "conservative" group, who preferred to die rather than fight on Sabbath, anticipated the sect of the Essenes, who believed this world is doomed and who yearned for the world to come.

In the midst of all this, around 150 BCE a group of Essenes, convinced that the priesthood of the temple administration was illegitimate and corrupt, fled to the Judean wilderness at Qumran to establish a community where they could live in ritual purity and prepare for *Ha-Olam Ha-Ba'*, the "World to Come." Some of the scrolls from this community indicate that its origins may have been a dispute between a "wicked priest" and the "teacher of righteousness" who was assassinated. They also express a belief that the community and the world will soon end in a war between the Sons of Light (them) and the Sons of Darkness (everybody else led by the Romans). Other writings connote that these may be symbolic and liturgical rubrics, thus the community

A Jewish religious sect called the Essenes lived at Qumran.

and its scrolls are still not completely understood. At any rate, the Romans destroyed Qumran in 68 CE before traveling to Jerusalem to do the same there in 70 CE. Some of these Essenes may have fled for refuge to Masada, where a duplicate of a text discovered in the caves of Qumran was found ("Songs of the Sabbath Sacrifice").

In 1947, so the story goes, a Bedouin boy searching for a lost goat threw a stone into one of these caves along the Dead Sea, heard a jar breaking, and ran away, afraid of a desert jinn. But the Bedouin soon returned to discover the first three, and then four more jars: the original seven Dead Sea Scrolls. Three ended up in the hands of a Bethlehem cobbler/antiquities dealer called Kando, and four in the possession of the Metropolitan of the Syrian Orthodox St. Mark's monastery in Jerusalem. Professor Eleazar Sukenik of Hebrew University acquired the three from Bethlehem, and his son, Yigael Yadin, upon seeing an ad in the *Wall Street Journal*, managed the anonymous purchase of the Metropolitan's four scrolls for a mere $250,000. (Nobody, with the exception of Professor Sukenik and a few others, understood what the scrolls actually were in those days.)

This initial discovery in what became known as Cave 1 prompted the scurrying of Bedouin and scholars alike to the neighboring caves; and over the next several years, scrolls were discovered in eleven of them, some in jars, some in fragments. How did the scrolls come to be here? Cave 4, the most picturesque cave that adorns most Dead Sea Scrolls textbooks, appears to have been a library. Some scrolls may have been secured in jars and hidden from the Romans. Some may have been brought by priests from Jerusalem for safe-keeping when the Holy City was under attack. They comprise Old Testament biblical books (all but Esther), books from the Apocrypha and the Pseudepigrapha, commentaries, rules for the conduct of the Essene community, guidelines for the final apocalypse and the ideal Temple, and much, much more. Their value is their witness to the diversity of Jewish life and beliefs in the first centuries BCE/CE, as well as the details they provide about the Essene sect. We knew the sect existed due to the witness of Josephus, Philo of Alexandria, the Roman statesman Pliny, and early church historians, but we knew very little about it before the discovery of the scrolls.

The discovery of the scrolls led to the excavation of the plateau opposite them, where the ruins of this Essene community were

Judea

discovered. The Essenes appear to have been quite diverse. Some lived with their families, most likely in Essene neighborhoods within Jewish cities. Some had more "Zealot leanings," looking forward to the final battle with the Romans; while others were more comfortable with a symbolic struggle between ultimate good and evil. Some were hard-core and moved here to Qumran to "make a level highway in the wilderness for our God" (Isaiah 40:3). These Essenes were ascetic, apocalyptic, and largely celibate. (Though there are also women and children buried in the cemetery.)

The Qumran community grew to three hundred. Since they were priestly and obsessed with ritual purity (to be ready for the world to come), they bathed in the ritual baths (mikvehs) daily. They also shared ritual meals (bread, wine, and sometimes ritually prepared meat) that did not include the sacrifices made at the Jerusalem Temple, which in their view were tainted by the illegitimate priesthood presiding there. They evidently lived in tents, huts, and caves around the excavated community center. An average day included rising early in the morning and doing one's physical labor (farming, hunting, pottery, laundry, and so on). Then, about noon, there was a ritual bath followed by a ritual meal, and the afternoon was spent in scholarly activity, including writing and copying the scrolls that they left behind. (Be sure to view a selection of the scrolls at the Shrine of the Book within the Israel Museum in Jerusalem.)

Begin your tour of the site by watching the brief and informative multimedia presentation opposite the entrance booth. The movie raises the question of whether John the Baptist had any connection with, or was perhaps even a member of, the Qumran Essene community. Matthew explicitly, and Mark implicitly, locates at least part of John's baptizing ministry at the Jordan River in the Judean wilderness just north of Qumran (Mark 1:9).[54] The Baptist and the Essenes shared an apocalyptic theology. They saw themselves as the fulfillment of Isaiah 40:3 ("Clear the LORD's way in the desert! Make a level highway in the wilderness for our God!"), and all four Gospels apply that passage to John the Baptist. Obviously, both thought baptism was extremely important; both were ascetics. It is likely that John knew of and perhaps participated in their rituals, but then decided that their message was too important to be kept exclusively to themselves and should be shared with the Jewish

Judea

communities throughout Israel: the time is at hand; a big event is in the making, and all Israel should know and be ready.

Upon exiting the multimedia presentation, turn sharply to the right and walk to the roofed area with seating. There you will see a sign facing the caves that points out Cave 1, where it all began. Then, utilizing the national park brochure map, make your way to "1. Aqueduct Entrance," which lies just up the path leading toward the caves. Usually, mikvehs contain either two sets of stairs or a divider, so that the bather goes down ritually impure and exits on the opposite side purified. Therefore, most of the larger pools without such divisions must be cisterns for water storage.

If you look from where you are standing up to the top of the cliffs, you may see water stains at the top of the wadi. When it rains in the winter, water pours down the valley slope of this wadi and is captured by the canal system built by the community, supplying mikvehs and cisterns with water. Follow the boarded path through the site, observing explanatory signs along the way. Make a left to "4. Tower," from which you can view the scriptorium, the long narrow building that was probably two stories. Descend the tower to enter the scriptorium, where there is an illustrative diagram. On your way you will pass a small room on your right, which was likely the meeting room of the leadership of the community. Note the plastered hole/channel in the wall through which water could be poured and messages could be passed when the ruling council sat in closed session.

Exiting and turning left takes you past the refectory, where the community held their "communion meal" of bread and wine, all the way to another roofed overlook, from which you can view the famous Cave 4 (pictured here). Head back toward the excavation and continue on the boarded path

Cave 4

Judea

past a huge mikveh with a serious crack in its floor, probably caused by the 31 BCE earthquake that resulted in a twenty-five-year hiatus in the settlement. Before exiting to the restrooms, gift shop, and restaurant, walk east of the excavation to view the cemetery and note that all the graves face toward Jerusalem: all the better to see the messiah(s) when he or they come.[55]

En Gedi (National Park)

When David fled from Saul to hide here in the tenth century BCE (1 Samuel 24), En Gedi was uninhabited. But in the seventh century BCE, Judean kings founded a town here that lasted until the Babylonian exile. While resettlement during the Persian period did not endure, the Hasmoneans (second century BCE) made the oasis a royal estate and administrative center. Sadly, Zealots from Masada invaded En Gedi to steal agricultural supplies during Passover in 68 CE and slaughtered more than seven hundred women and children. However, a vibrant Jewish community was reborn here during the third through sixth centuries CE, until it was destroyed by Byzantine Christianity's own brand of zealotry. Jews returned to En Gedi in 1949, settled in 1953, and the kibbutz was founded three years later.

The draws to this magnificent place are the same today as then: date farms atop a gorgeous view, the therapeutic waters of the Dead Sea, the low altitude with its mineral-enriched atmosphere, the cultivation of aromatic plants (such as the ancient persimmon/balsam for perfumes), and medicinal herbs. In Song of Songs 1:14, the lovers celebrate the henna blossoms of En Gedi; and Ezekiel 47 envisions the restorative waters flowing from the Temple Mount by way of the Kidron Valley into the Dead Sea, to freshen its waters at En Gedi during the dawn of the messianic age.

The ancient synagogue is accessible to all. Discovered accidentally by the kibbutz in 1965, the site's excavations began in 1970 and are ongoing. The *bet kneset*, as it is called in Hebrew, the spiritual and communal center of Jewish life, was begun in the third century CE atop the ruins of the Second Temple period Jewish community that lived here. It stood, through expansions and renovations, until the sixth century CE. Follow the national park brochure route past a mikveh, basin, and into the synagogue, which is oriented toward

Judea

Jerusalem by the holy ark housing the Torah scroll in the north wall. Just behind the ark is a tiny *geniza* (storeroom for worn-out writings). Just beside that is the Seat of Moses, and just in front is the bimah from which the Torah was read. Stepped rows of seats are on the facing south wall. Columns form three aisles surrounding a central mosaic.

This synagogue is more conservative than its Galilean counterparts in that it depicts no human or Greco-Roman mythological images, but only leaves, birds, peacocks, grapes, menorahs, and geometric designs. Similarly, the Hebrew and Aramaic inscriptions in the mosaic floor of the western aisle (described in detail in the park brochure) include the motif of the zodiac popular in Byzantine/Talmudic-era synagogues, but only by listing their names without their signs, along with biblical characters and blessings. Most interesting and unique is a "curse" or warning in the third panel: "Anyone causing a controversy between a man and his friend, or whoever slanders his friend before the Gentiles, or whoever reveals the secret of the town to the Gentiles—He whose eyes range through the whole earth and Who sees hidden things, He will set his face on that man and on his seed and will uproot him from under the heavens. And all the people said: Amen and Amen Selah."[56] The mysterious secret was the key to the town's economic welfare: the distilling of a rare and intoxicating perfume from the ancient persimmon/balsam plant.

The entrance to Nakhal (Wadi) David is separate from that of the synagogue, but also on the national parks ticket. There is absolutely no smoking or eating in the park, and as always in Israel's nature reserves, respect the flora by looking but not picking and respect the fauna by being quiet. Going early might avoid large groups of Israeli schoolkids. The first part of the walk up the wadi is wheelchair-accessible and should be enjoyed by all. It goes up to the first waterfall. Then the hike begins, up many stairs cut into the rock and passing by several other gorgeous waterfalls produced by David's Spring. The entire hike up to David's Falls and back to where you started is a circular path that takes about an hour and a half, which includes some rest stops for enjoying the scenery.

If you have more time and the athletic ability, on the return loop from David's Falls, make a sharp right on the trail to the En

Gedi Spring and walk up to the Chalcolithic (Copper Age) temple (ca. 3000 BCE). Serving as a central shrine for desert peoples before there was a town here, it is amazingly typical of the ancient Near Eastern temple design that extended into the biblical period: a courtyard around a central basin leads to a rectangular temple building with an altar, where ash and animal bones were found, centered against the rear wall. Even if you are not an archaeology buff, the view from here is amazing. Numerous other hikes of varying difficulty are outlined clearly in the nature reserve brochure, including nearby Wadi Arugot, with its own entrance kiosk. Keep in mind sunset times and that entrance to the nature reserve may not be allowed if you arrive less than two hours before closing time.

Ibex at Kibbutz En Gedi

Without a doubt the place to stay to get the most out of your experience of the Judean wilderness is the Kibbutz En Gedi Guest House, adjacent to the national park and within the nature reserve (phone: 08-659-4222; website: www.ein-gedi.co.il/en). *En Gedi* means "Spring of the Kid," and the indigenous mountain goat, the ibex, may greet you on your way to dinner or on the putt-putt golf course or beside the pool. Local coneys, or rock badgers, scamper along the remote paths outside the guesthouse campus, which is replete with local and migrating birds and more than one thousand varieties of flora in one of the world's finest botanical gardens. A tour of the garden is available that includes the history of the kibbutz and a commentary on the future of the kibbutz movement. This is also the best place to experience and enjoy the healthy gifts of the Dead Sea, its minerals and blood pressure–lowering altitude, through a swim, baths, and numerous massage options. Schedule at least one free day! (The Kibbutz Guest House does not accept group reservations for less than two nights.)

Masada (National Park)

This natural fortress was first fortified by the Hasmoneans, probably by High Priest Alexander Jannaeus (103–76 BCE), to help protect their southern border. But Herod the Great discovered its value during his power struggle with them and acquired it for his winter palace, where he would be safe if either the Jews or the Romans turned against him. Upon his death in 4 BCE, his son Archelaus ruled Judah

Herod's Northern Palace

for only ten years. So in 6 CE, the family palace passed to the direct control of the Roman procurator. But at the beginning of the First Jewish Revolt in the summer of 66 CE, it came under the control of the Zealots. The most fanatical of this sect were the Sicarii, so called after the *sica*, or curved dagger, which was their trademark weapon, led by a certain Menahem ben Judah the Galilean. The disciple of Jesus who eventually betrayed him was Judas Iscariot, that is, Judah of the Sicarii. And these Galilean associations with the Zealot movement may have been what prompted Nathanael's quip to Philip when first hearing of Jesus: "Can anything from Nazareth be good?" (John 1:46). Judas's disenchantment with Jesus' messiahship was possibly that it did not live out his Zealot expectations for the violent overthrow of Rome.

Menahem was assassinated in Jerusalem in 66 CE, and his relative Eleazar ben Jair escaped to Masada to lead the group there, which was evidently joined by fellow Zealots who fled Jerusalem upon its destruction in 70 CE. In 73 or 74 CE, the Tenth Roman Legion, led by Flavius Silva, besieged Masada with the aid of eight thousand troops in eight camps surrounding the mountain, which are still visible from above as diamond-shaped formations. After

Judea

> **The land around Masada still shows where the Tenth Roman Legion camped.**

a few months, the Romans managed to breach the wall with a ramp on the western, most vulnerable side. As to what happened next, we have only the witness of Josephus, who says he based his account on the accounts of two women and five children who hid themselves away in cisterns.

Josephus says that the Romans breached the wall on the eve of Passover (fifteenth of Nissan) when there was a full moon, and then retired to wait until morning. During this time, Eleazar ben Jair gave a spirited speech that led the 960 members of the community to draw lots, whereby every father killed his family. Then ten men killed all the fathers, and one man killed the ten and committed suicide. Josephus himself had been a Zealot in the Galilee who surrendered to the Romans. He wrote in Rome and could have consulted with Flavius Silva, who was there in 81 CE. But he did not have firsthand knowledge, and there are errors in his description of the site. Based on other records of Roman invasion, it is incredible that Silva would have breached the wall in full moon and then gone to bed. Eleazar's speech has been cast by Josephus to appeal to the heroic instincts of his Roman audience and, if it occurred at all, probably was delivered earlier. We do have the evidence of the lots found near the synagogue and mentioned below. It may be that a group agreed to commit suicide, some fought to the death, and perhaps only those fortunate widows and orphans survived in the cisterns to tell the story. The mountain solitude that remained attracted a cluster of desert monks in the fifth century CE, with thirteen cells around a chapel built by Euthymius.

For your visit, allow at least half a day. As a general rule, it is best to begin first thing in the morning. Do not go if rain is expected, as the Dead Sea highway (90) often floods, and visitors have been stranded overnight. Around the circular entrance hall are restrooms, a kiosk to buy bottled water, and the ticket counter where you can use your national parks ticket. Be sure to get the detailed site brochure. The cable car is an extra charge, and tickets can be purchased for round-trip or one way. There is a snake path for walking: up takes about an hour, and down takes about half an hour. If you are with a group, a good plan is to require all to take the cable car up and then to let the athletic descend by foot. Winter weather can be cold and windy at the top, and in the summer it is extremely hot. In both cases a water bottle is a must, and there are places to fill it on the mountaintop. A food court at the base (where both the cable car and the snake path conclude) can provide lunch, which is also available at nearby En Bokek (south) or En Gedi Spa (north).

After viewing the historical video (just up the stairs from the ticket counter), begin on top of the mountain at the guardhouse. You can see the benches around you that were beautifully plastered walls made to look like marble. The black line is the "in situ line": below it is the area that was found in place by the archaeologists; the area above it has been reconstructed. Keep in mind throughout your walking tour that you are viewing only what remains after two thousand years. Imagine tall walls and buildings, frescoes and marbled edifices, fruit tree groves among vegetable gardens and dovecotes. Imagine a luxurious palace complex, a desert oasis, built by King Herod the Great. Take a sharp right and head up the path past a rock quarry that later became a dry moat protecting Herod's Northern Palace. Directly across and to the right is the palace governor/commander's residence, also protecting the entrance to Herod's private family palace complex. You can enter this by continuing forward up the path. Pass through the many storerooms, for such items as grain, wine, and dried fruits, to the bathhouse (a sharp left).

The Roman bath was a staple of society, and Herod was thoroughly Roman in this regard. In the dressing room are still visible parts of the tile floor and frescoed walls (the Zealots built a mikveh in the corner). Then immediately before you is the tepidarium (warm bath) with the frigidarium (cold bath) to the right and the caldarium (hot bath) to the left. In the latter, note how the floor was built upon short pillars, under which the furnace on the far end (a cave-shaped Plexiglas today) forced hot air that also traveled up the terra-cotta piping in the walls (partially reconstructed for you in the corner). The exit is an artificial one through the wall to expedite traffic, so walk out and around through the long storage room again to ascend to the personal residence of Herod himself.

Judea

The rock glacis provided extra security after the dry moat and commandant's residence. You will first meet the family dwelling area, which overlooks on a semicircular balcony a magnificent view to the north. Below you are visible two other rooms: a circular "den," surrounded by double columns and perhaps used for entertaining; and below that the "Jacuzzi room," with a small bath, overlooking the Judean wilderness and the mountains of Moab to the east.

Retrace your steps back toward the bathhouse, but turn right. There you will see a series of steps going down to the "den" and "Jacuzzi room," and opposite the steps a benched, covered seating area. The able-bodied can go down; others can sit and rest. When all are rejoined, proceed right through the little seating room to the "room of the lots," where were found potsherds with names of members of the Zealots, including Ben Jair, commander of the Sacarii.

Retrace your steps once again back through the seating room in the shade, and turn a sharp left past the "water gate" and through another guardroom similar to the one you first entered after the cable car ride up. Veer to the right past a cistern to see an interactive demonstration of how Herod's engineers collected his water: small cisterns around the mountain were fed by channels that forwarded winter floodwaters into them. Fill the pitcher with water from the faucet to demonstrate. Then continue the circle around to the synagogue.

Scholars debate whether this room was originally a synagogue built for Herod's staff or a room of another use, converted by the Zealots as they did the dining room at the Herodium. Regardless, the Zealots added at least the *geniza* (storeroom for worn-out writings), in which was found a fragment of Ezekiel 37, the vision of the dry bones, which must have served as inspiration for the Zealots. If Ben Jair gave a speech at all, this would have been in the place. Exit to the right past dovecoats (doves were raised for food) and enter one of the casemate walls, in which were found other scrolls, for a premier view of the Roman ramp that breached the western wall of Masada.

Walking on to the south past the ramp, take a sharp left into the fifth-century CE chapel of the Byzantine monks. Interesting is the crypt or reliquary beneath the altar, the grapes and breadbasket motif in the mosaic floor, and the "rock mosaic" decoration on the walls.

Exit south to the "Western Palace," which served as the public building of governance for King Herod. Walk through the guard room, formal hall, and another guardroom to an entrance hall, before which is a throne room (four depressions in the floor mark the throne of Herod). Going up the stairs will bring you to the bath complex of this palace, which was more for "public guests" and not those close to the Herodian family.

> Josephus was a captured Jewish commander and Pharisee who defected to the Roman side and later wrote major books about Jewish history.

Walk down from the gorgeous mosaics via another set of stairs, past some bathtubs and what could have been a latrine, to the huge public swimming pool straight ahead. Farther beyond is the Bet Midrash, or House of (Torah) Study, built probably by the Zealots. The hearty should keep walking south to the end of the plateau to see a second swimming pool. (Note the steps and how the Zealots again built a mikveh in the corner.) The pièce de résistance of the whole mountaintop, for those who have come this far, is the "mother of all cisterns": Masada's chief cistern, to which slaves would have transported water from the numerous mini-cisterns around the mountain complex.

Return to the cable car or snake path and descend for a much-deserved lunch at the site, En Gedi, or En Bokek.

★ Dead Sea

This lowest body of water on earth is called *Yam Hamelakh* (Salt Sea) in Hebrew, and the Romans called it the Lake of Asphalt. The term "Dead Sea" was first used in the second century CE. It is actually quite alive with healing minerals, and people with skin diseases flock here from all over the world. The low altitude is also good for the heart.[57] It is more than thirteen hundred feet below sea level, but it was forty feet higher at the beginning of the twentieth century. Sadly, the water level continues to drop dramatically each year due to the siphoning off of its natural supply from the Sea of Galilee (for drinking and irrigation), damming up of the wadis, water use by the cosmetic industry on the southern shore, and climate change.

Judea

Students at the Dead Sea

This large salt lake lies in the basin of the Great Rift Valley. This valley extends from the base of Mount Hermon (ca. 9,000 feet above sea level), down the Hula Valley, through the Sea of Galilee and the Jordan River, and beyond the Dead Sea farther south to the Aravah Valley, the Red Sea, and even into Africa. This geological fault accounts for the many earthquakes in the region from biblical times until today. The top of Masada is a bit over 100 feet above sea level, and Jerusalem rests upon the Judean hills at ca. 2,700 feet above sea level. When you descend from Jerusalem to the Dead Sea (or Jericho), you drop about 4,000 feet, which explains why your ears pop! The sea itself is a vast 1,000 feet deep, though it is drying up rapidly.[58]

The water of the Dead Sea is seven times more dense than seawater. It is over 30 percent salt, and therefore ten times saltier than the ocean. It is fatal to the lungs and will blind the eyes. Enter slowly and then sit gently, as if in your recliner at home. If you are not obese, you may roll over onto your stomach in the water. You can paddle around, but you should *not* swim. This

> **The Dead Sea is therapeutic, but don't get any water in your eyes.**

is not the ocean. If you get Dead Sea water in your eyes, have a friend pour fresh water into your eyes immediately. Be especially careful if the weather is windy, as currents can carry you out farther. Wear something on your feet to avoid cuts from the salt bottom.

Hebron

According to Genesis 23, Abraham purchased the Cave of Machpelah here for his family burial grounds, although Rachael was buried en route farther north at Rāmah (not the traditional site at Bethlehem).[59] Herod built a massive and impressive edifice on the site, comparable to his Temple renovations in Jerusalem. There were subsequent Muslim modifications. The modern history of Hebron (or Kiryat Arba) is stressed. A Jewish community resided here until 1929 when they were slaughtered by Arabs. It is now the home of almost one hundred thousand Arabs who have resisted the return of Jews since the 1967 Six-Day War. Because of the unsettledness of the situation, at least at this writing, tour leaders should weigh group visitation soberly. If you go, a visit to one of the local glassblowing establishments is recommended. You will find the Palestinians a loving and beautiful people trying to live among Jews who also legitimately claim a heritage from their mutual father, Abraham.

Judea

Israelis and Bedouin shopping south of Hebron

NOTES

NOTES

NOTES

Central and Southern Negev

Tel Be'er Sheva (National Park)

Also known as: Beersheba

Be'er Sheva means "Seven Wells," but the word for "seven" also means "to swear," so the name can connote "Well of Swearing." In an apparent etiology, Abraham swore an oath here with Abimelech after arguing over the use of a well (Genesis 21:22-34). Isaac built an altar here (Genesis 26:12-33); and Jacob had a vision here before taking his family to Egypt (Genesis 46:1-7). It was recorded as part of the tribe of Simeon after the exodus, and then of Judah. The corrupt sons of Samuel judged here (1 Samuel 8:1-3); and David made it the fortress, parallel with Arad to the east, guarding the southern border of his kingdom. It was destroyed by Pharaoh Shishak in 925 BCE, but it was rebuilt and became a prosperous Israelite city in the ninth–eighth centuries BCE. The prophet Amos condemned northern Israelites for making pilgrimages to the temple at Be'er Sheva,

Israelite four-room house

and in fact, in the excavations the altar was found broken in pieces, an act probably attributable to King Hezekiah (eighth century BCE) or Josiah (seventh century BCE). Second Kings 23:7 reports that "the king tore down the shrines" (temples with their altars) outside Jerusalem. The town sits just south of Hebron at the end of the Judean hill country, the ridge of mountains that runs up the backbone of Israel becoming the Ephraimite hill country in Samaria. It provides the gateway to the Negev (south) desert.

Opposite the entrance kiosk, where you are required to put on helmets, is a reproduction of the altar mentioned above (the original is in the Israel Museum) and a sitting area for group discussions. Note that the tamarisk trees mentioned in the Bible are popular here because of the underground water. Take the path up to the tel and pause at the restored well just outside the gate of the Israelite Iron Age city. Survey the landscape. Abraham, Isaac, and Jacob were seminomads. This means they farmed their ancestral land during the winter rainy season, but in the summer, after letting their flocks finish off the harvested fields of wheat and barley, they picked up their tents and moved on to find grazing grounds in the wadis. When fall came, they returned to their ancestral property to plant more wheat and barley, which you may be able to observe in the Bedouin farms lying before you.

Enter the city through its gate. Ahead was the governor's mansion, and to the right were the city's storage rooms. Walk left past the many Israelite homes built into the casemate wall: an entryway leading to an open courtyard with the roofed barn to the right and living quarters straight ahead. Note a room thirteen feet below the surface on the right-hand side of the street. Because of its depth and intersecting perpendicular walls, this was probably the location of the shrine that King Hezekiah or Josiah destroyed. An observation tower in the midst of the tel allows an overview. Heading back toward the entrance gate, don't exit there but turn left to the in-town water system that brought secure and convenient water within the city walls. Exit carefully through it and emerge outside, where you can view the ingenious engineering that brought rainwater from the desert flash floods into the water system. There is a Negev museum at the site. If you have the time and interest, you might want to ask the officials to open it for you.

Tel Arad (National Park)

The earliest mention of Arad in the Bible refers to this area (Numbers 21:1: "the Canaanite king of Arad, who ruled in the arid southern plain"). And Judges 1:16 recalls that the descendants of Moses' Midianite/Kenite father-in-law came up with the Israelites from Jericho and settled here. King David protected his southern border and the road to Elat and Edom by building an unwalled military outpost here, at the center of which stood a shrine and an altar. Solomon turned it into a fortified citadel with a temple. Pharaoh Shishak destroyed it in 925 BCE, five years after Solomon's death, but it was rebuilt by Solomon's son Rehoboam and refortified by subsequent kings of Judah.

From the entrance gate, where there are restrooms, drive up to the Israelite citadel. If you have a bus driver, have him return to the lower parking lot. The city gate has been reconstructed; note the in situ line. Walk in and straight up the Hellenistic tower in the center for an overview of the site. To the north you can see where the Judean hills end at Hebron and the Negev begins. In the opposite direction (southwest), the large sprawling city you can see is modern Arad. The most interesting aspect of this tel is Solomon's

Solomon's Temple

> All temples in the ancient Near East are built on an east-west axis.

temple, which appears before you as it had been altered by the end of the ninth century BCE. The entrance faces east, as at Solomon's Temple in Jerusalem. The largest portion is the exterior courtyard where worshipers gathered around what was originally a central altar. Additional rooms for the priests were added, adjoining the courtyard.

The altar was built by the specifications of Israel's oldest law code[60] (after the Ten Commandments) in Exodus 20:25-26 and in Deuteronomy 27:5-6, of unhewn stones, without a series of steps leading up to it, in order to distinguish it from Canaanite altars. The four top cornerstones provided the "horns of the altar," which were clearly visible in the 1990s but are now worn by erosion. A channel carved in the central rock atop the altar where the sacrifice was placed allowed the blood to flow downward, probably into the basin below.[61] The altar was covered and put out of operation by Hezekiah's reform in the eighth century BCE, and then the entire temple was filled with debris during Josiah's seventh-century BCE reform to close down temples/shrines other than what had become the authentic one in Jerusalem on Mount Zion, God's holy mountain and abode.

West of the altar, only priests would enter the building, which is elongated north-south instead of east-west as its larger and grander Jerusalem counterpart. In the center, the holy of holies is built into the west wall, flanked by incense altars that still had ash in them when found.[62] Also found here was one (left side) *matsevah*, standing stone. There is a clear depression in the wall, however, indicating that it had at an earlier period a mate on the right. Deuteronomy 27:5-6, referenced above, continues in verse 8 to say, "Make sure to write all the words of this Instruction on the stones plainly and clearly." The *matsevah* standing on the left had its sides smoothed and painted red. Monumental tables, such as those described here, are not always actually inscribed with the laws but stand as representative of them. It is tempting to speculate that Solomon might have set up two standing stones as representative of the two tablets of the law.

Exit the temple gate through which you entered, and turn left to the overlook of the early Bronze Age city, 2,900–2,700 BCE. As you can see, it was massive, enclosed by the city wall-tower complex round about. Continue around the top of the tel to the left, back to the Hellenistic tower where you began. Descend out the Arad city gate you first entered, and turn right to descend down to the lower city. Follow the path into the lower city, which of course predated by many years the Israelite citadel. As you enter, you'll first see the temple complex on the right, with its altar and basin, not substantially different from the Israelite one. The palace is across the street. Along the street you can see a reconstructed home: a rectangular building with a bench around it and an oven outside. This is exactly the architecture of Bedouin tents, leading one to suspect that the early Bronze Age desert Bedouins, as they formed their earliest cities, built their homes on the models of their forefathers' tents. Curiously, these homes are all below ground level, presumably because this made them cooler in the summer and warmer in the winter when rains were diverted by their water collection system.

This brings you around and down to the cistern, which explains why there was a primitive city here in the first place. The limestone in this area is impervious to water. Peer down the shaft, and at the bottom is dark stone, a remnant of the original Canaanite reservoir. The Israelites built the well, and the gray stone just up from the black stone is evidence of that. The yellowish stone is Herodian. The Israelites used the Canaanite technology and carried the water by pack animals up the hill to the citadel and deposited it in a channel, which then carried it into the citadel cistern adjacent to the temple.

Walk on down the path exiting the Bronze Age city to meet your transportation. A picnic area is provided to the left. Commercial lunch places are available in the mall in the modern city of Arad. In Arad you will also find the Arad Museum and Visitors Center, 28 Ben Yair Street, displaying the artifacts from the site's archaeological excavations.

Central and Southern Negev

En Avdat (National Park)

This breathtaking hike through nature's artwork is about one hour south of Be'er Sheva on Highway 40, which continues on to Mitzpe Ramon. It is possible to visit Arad, Be'er Sheva, En Avdat, and Avdat from Jerusalem, but it makes for a very long and tiring day. It is better to stay at the Kibbutz En Gedi Guest House for two to five days as your home base from which to explore the area we today call the central Negev. If you are game for a little adventure, you can overnight at the guest house overlooking En Avdat at Midreshet Sde Boker (www.boker.org.il/english/). The sunsets and sunrises are incomparable!

Begin the hike at the lower parking lot on the northern end of the park, exiting Highway 40 between kilometer markers 130 and 131 per the sign toward Midreshet Sde Boker. Restrooms and picnic tables are provided at the entrance. If you and your group walk silently, you will hear and see more wildlife, especially the birds and the ibex, to whom the Bible says God has given these mountainous slopes (Psalm 104:18). The ibex live in separate male and female herds except during the mating season from September to November. The bucks are larger with longer horns and a full beard. The does give birth to one or two kids in the spring. As you walk, note how the limestone is layered with the black flint, creating a lovely natural mosaic. The climb out of the canyon is challenging, but it is possible to walk up to the waterfall and then return to the lower parking lot entrance. Those who are able will want to walk all the way up and out to the upper (south) parking lot between Highway 40 kilometer markers 123 and 124, where your transportation should meet you and where restrooms are also available.

Not far down the trail, a huge solitary 250-year-old Atlantic terebinth rises on the left, testimony to a time when more rain fell here in the Wilderness of Zin. At the northern end of the path is a delightful grove of Mesopotamian poplars. The way up and out of the canyon is by many stairs and a few ladders. Near the top are caves that housed Byzantine monks. It is not allowed to begin your hike at the upper parking lot and walk down; the trail is one-way only.

As you experience the beauty and solitude of this area, you

Graves of David and Paula Ben-Gurion

may appreciate why David Ben-Gurion, father and first prime minister of Israel, chose to retire here with his beloved wife, Paula. He always said that the future of Israel was in the South (Negev), and he believed in the biblical prophecy of Isaiah that the desert would again bloom. Their home at Kibbutz Sde Boker can be toured, and their tombs at Midreshet Sde Boker can also be visited. It is Jewish custom to place a small stone on the graves as evidence of visitation and respect.

Avdat (National Park)

The Nabataean kingdom, with its capital in Petra (modern Jordan), held sway here from roughly the third century BCE to the second century CE when they became absorbed into the Roman Empire, and subsequently the Byzantine Empire. With the Muslim conquest of the area in the seventh century CE, Avdat ceased to exist. The Nabataeans were originally tent dwellers, and this was an outpost protecting their "Spice Route" from Arabia to the Mediterranean. Gradually they turned to agriculture and animal husbandry and began to build more permanent structures. Rainfall in this region is minimal, so farming depends on capturing every drop. Modern examples of this can be observed along the highways

Cruciform baptistery

in the Negev where the Israelis have created pockets to catch the rainwater and plant groves of trees. Reconstructions of a Nabataean farm are available near Avdat and at Shivta farther south.

To visit, stop first at the lowest parking lot to view an informative video about the Nabataeans at the welcome center. There are also a couple of eating establishments by the adjacent filling station (although some prefer to bring a picnic lunch to En Avdat). You should use the restrooms at the portal to the ascent road as there are none up the hill. On the way up, on the right, are the Roman cemetery and villa. At the upper parking lot, begin the walking trail with the Roman tower, which should be ascended for the view. Walk through the Roman housing area, diverting to the right to the Nabataean pottery shop, and retracing your steps to enter the Byzantine fortress where you can walk to the eastern tower to view the ruins of the Nabatean army camp.

The Byzantine Christians built their church complex over the Nabataean temple. You'll pass the Church of St. Theodore first on the left. Then proceed farther to the earlier excellent example of a fourth-century CE church of a single apse, the steps of which mount the bishop's seat with square rooms on either side housing reliquaries. Exit farther to view the cruciform baptismal font.

The small basin might have been for infants. Keep going down the stairs past the Byzantine storage and housing area, at the end of which is a restored house with its cave storage rooms (including grain and wine) in the rear. Your driver should meet you here at the intermediate parking lot. Reachable by foot from here or from the lowest parking lot (near the filling station) is the best example of a Byzantine bathhouse in Israel.

Wilderness of Zin

Mamshit (National Park)

A bit more remote to the east is another Nabataean outpost. The visit is self-guided by the provided signs. Mamshit's claim to fame is the oldest Christian church in the central Negev, the so-called East Church built before 427 CE. We find two crosses in the mosaic floor there, and crosses were forbidden in church floors after this date. As at the Avdat early church, this church has only one apse with reliquary rooms on either side. Touching the bones of the saints was important in the early church, as kissing the traditional slab where Jesus' body was prepared for burial is important for Eastern Rite Christians today. The cruciform baptistery is exquisite, with steps on three sides and a depression to hold a pitcher of water.

Makhtesh Ramon

Mitzpe Ramon

Nestled roughly between the biblical wildernesses of Zin and Paran, in what Israelis today call the central Negev, the Ramon Visitor Center and Bio Ramon (National Park) overlook the amazing Makhtesh Ramon (Ramon Crater). The visitor center explains how this geological wonder was formed. From there you can explore the crater on your own or hire any number of touring options. If you would like to stay overnight in the area, Mitzpe Ramon is your best choice because you are in the middle of nowhere! What better way to experience a taste of the Israelites "wandering in the wilderness"?

Har Karkom (Mount Sinai?)

There are about twelve scholarly proposals for where Mount Sinai was located. This is one of them. One thing is for sure: it was a holy mountain for someone. There are twelve standing stones (tribes of Israel?) at the foot of the mountain and a cleft in the rock at the summit from which Moses could have observed God's glory pass by (Exodus 33:22). Rock art depicts a snake (Numbers 21:8-9), what appear to be two stone tablets (Ten Commandments?), a (burning?) bush, and more. This is a full-day desert experience, from dawn to dusk, but there is nothing like it in the world!

Cleft of the rock

You cannot visit this site on your own. Har Karkom is in a military firing zone, and so it can only be reached on Shabbat by camel or jeep. You can arrange a jeep tour with an Israeli guide at www.negevjeep.co.il/english/; groups will need reservations. Arrive at Mitzpe Ramon on Friday for an overnight stay in order to travel from there to the mountain early Saturday morning by jeep, enjoy a lengthy guided walking tour, and return by jeep in the evening. To prepare for your visit, study the materials at www.harkarkom.com.[63]

Timna Park and Elat

Timna is about thirty minutes north of Elat (on Highway 90), and the two locations could not be more different: think Israelite desert spirituality versus Canaanite urban decadence, and you won't be far off. To visit Timna Park, you need at least half a day, and it could fill an entire day if you have the time. One good plan is to do Timna first thing in the morning and spend the afternoon in Elat.

Timna is traditionally called Solomon's Mines because of the abundant supply of copper in its soil, and, indeed, the modern Israeli copper mines are adjacent to the park entrance. At the entrance booth, it is recommended that you purchase the entire package. Begin there with the 360-degree audiovisual presentation on the

Timna

geology and history of the mines. Then begin your tour using the map supplied in the park brochure. Go first to "Solomon's Pillars" and park there. Walk to the right of them to the "Hathor Temple."

What makes Timna so interesting is that it brings us to the heart of Mosaic exodus religion and how it differs from Egyptian royal religion. Obviously the copper mines were extremely valuable in the thirteenth–eleventh centuries BCE, and the archaeological evidence here shows a struggle between the urban Egyptian and the desert Midianite cultures. The latter is intimately connected to the origins of Israelite religion. Moses benefited from the patronage of his father-in-law, Jethro, a Midianite priest; and recent scholarship traces the origins of the name of the Israelite God, YHWH, to the Midianite Shasu, who worshiped the God Yahu/YHW (*u* and *w* are the same letter). *Yahu* actually occurs in many early Israelite names such as Eliyahu (Elijah), "my God is Yahu"; Yesha'yahu (Isaiah), "Yahu saves"; and Yahu-akhaz (King Ahaz), "Yahu has grasped."

Smelting was a sacred

> **Recent scholarship connects the Israelite God YHWH to the Midianite god YHW.**

activity in the ancient world. Much like agriculture, in which the miracle of a seed becoming a plant was blessed by sacred ritual, so the change of earth's soil into a precious metal was a religious enterprise. The first operations here were guarded, giving way gradually to a peaceful coexistence between the Egyptians and the Midianites. By the eleventh century BCE, the original Egyptian presence had given way to the Midianite.

Stand in front of the temple and observe. Hathor was the Egyptian divine cow who gave birth each day to Horus the sun god. Also called "the Lady of Turquoise," she was divine patron of the turquoise mines in the central Sinai Peninsula and therefore venerated here. The temple was under Egyptian control from about 1300 to 1150 BCE. During this period, the central niche was framed on either side by pillars with Hathor heads. When the Midianites took over, they cut the heads of Hathor off the pillars and reused one or both of them by placing them upside down along the left wall in a row of standing stones, the desert religion's iconoclastic representation of divine presence.[64] Archaeologists found rolls of heavy red and yellow cloth along the walls of the temple, evidence that a Midianite tabernacle covered the sanctuary similar to the one described in the Torah as associated with the exodus event. Ascend the steps to the right and view through a "telescope" the hieroglyphic inscription of Ramses III offering a sacrifice to Hathor. Continue up the steps through the arch for a magnificent view, and then journey down to Solomon's Pillars. (This walk is challenging, and some pilgrims may prefer to return from the temple low ground directly to the Solomon's Pillars area and to your transportation in the parking lot.)

Proceed to the "Mushroom Camp," which was undefended and therefore dates to the later period when the Egyptians and the Midianites were at peace. The tour is self-guided using the signs. Walk forward to the smelting pits and then farther to the Midianite temple, where again we observe only a line of standing stones behind an altar. Walking toward the

> Copper has been an essential material to humanity since prehistoric times.

"mushroom" formation, note the furnace with its explanation of the smelting operation.

Travel on to the parking lot of the "Ancient Mines and Arches." The former can be observed by means of the mine shafts dug deep into the earth to extract the copper, some of which is usually visible at the surface as turquoise-green sand particles. The energetic can hike on to the beautiful "arches" if they wish.

Return to your transportation and drive to the "Chariots." At the far end of the walk, into a tunnel, the rock engravings may be instructive. Egyptian chariots and shielded warriors seem to compete with Midianite ibex, oryx, and, on the far left, a desert ostrich.

At the lake area there are restrooms, snacks and light lunch, activities for children, and a full-scale amateur model of the Tabernacle, which is interesting to walk through even with its mistakes, such as angels instead of cherubim (winged sphinxes).

In Elat there are numerous things to do. The beach shows you why it is called the Red Sea. It's not the water but the color of the sand. Just across to the east is the Jordanian city of Aqaba, and day tours to Petra can be reserved at your hotel. Scuba diving and snorkeling are favorite activities along the shore to the south, along with

Camels of Shaharut

windsurfing at Elat beaches. The Underwater Observatory Marine Park Eilat at Coral Beach (south of Elat; website: www.coralworld. com/eilat/eng/) is a great place to spend an afternoon. Food is available, as are submarine cruises. Several establishments in Coral Beach rent snorkeling equipment, and for scuba diving at all levels of expertise, visit DeepSiam (phone: 08-6323636; website: en.deepdivers. co.il).

If you plan to take an excursion to St. Catherine's Monastery in the Sinai, the crossing point is here at Taba, where on the Egyptian side hotels are cheaper. The place to stay at the traditional Mount Sinai is Morganland (www.morgenland-village.net). Your Elat hotel can also arrange a day trip to the monastery (which, however, will not allow time to climb the mountain).

Hai-Bar

Out-of-the-Way Desert Experiences

Hai-Bar Yotvata Nature Reserve (National Park)

Just north of Timna Park on Highway 90 is the perfect place to get up close to the fauna of the desert. It even has a special building for the night creatures, in which the lighting for a.m. and p.m. are reversed. So when you tour it during the day, the critters think it is actually night, and they are out and active!

Camel Riders at Shaharut

If you want more than a one-minute rip-off "camel ride" at a filling station, this is the destination for you! Camel Riders offers a diversity of experiences, such as a two-hour camel ride for those with limited time, or a four-hour ride that includes lunch in a Bedouin tent to make it a half-day experience. You can also stay overnight in a Bedouin tent or take multiday caravans (phone: 08-637-3218; their web page, www.camel-riders.com, is in Hebrew, but the contact information you'll need is in English). Directions are provided

Camel riders at Shaharut

on the web page. Just north of Hai-Bar on Highway 90 is Yotvata, where you turn west up the Shaharut ascent road. The young and colorful Israeli guides provide information (in English) about the way of life in the wilderness, including flora and fauna.

Shefela

Shefela

Interesting Places to See in the Shefela

The Shefela is the region of fertile rolling hills lying between the southern coastal (Philistine) plain (from Tel Aviv to Ashkelon) and the Judean hill country (crowned by Jerusalem). The farmer turned prophet, Micah, came from the Shefela (Moreshet-Gat[65]). This area can be visited as a day trip from your home base in Jerusalem, or on your way to or from Ben Gurion Airport.

Tel Gezer (National Park)

Gezer, in the northern Shefela, is an excellent place to begin or end your study tour of the Holy Land. From the word for "cut" in Hebrew, Gezer sits on the cutting edge between the ancient Via Maris and the road up to Jerusalem, hence its strategic importance. On a clear day you can see Tel Aviv and Ashkelon to the west and Jerusalem to the east, which gives you a good introduction or review of the geography of the Holy Land. North of Tel Aviv, the Sharon Plain reaches to Mount Carmel. To the east, observe how the gently rolling hills of the Shefela escalate to the mountains running

Standing stones at Gezer

up and down the backbone of the country: the Judean hills from Jerusalem south to Hebron; the Samaritan hills (Ephraimite hill country) north of Jerusalem up to the Galilee. South of Hebron is Be'er Sheva and the beginning of the Negev, which extends to the Red Sea (Gulf of Elat). Above the Jezreel Valley, which separates Samaria from Galilee, the rolling hills of Galilee (steeper than those of the Shefela) rise up to the Golan Heights and Mount Hermon on the Lebanese-Syrian border. East of the mountain spine running north-south from Galilee to the Negev is an elongated wilderness region up and down the Jordan River valley.

The Karnak temple (in Luxor, Egypt) boasts that Pharaoh Thutmose III defeated Gezer in about 1466 BCE, and it remained a vassal Canaanite city-state under Egyptian domination throughout the fourteenth century BCE, as documented by the Amarna letters. Pharaoh Merneptah found it necessary to reestablish control in 1230 BCE, after which he named himself the "Binder of Gezer." Pharaoh Siamun gave Solomon his daughter in marriage, and Gezer was her dowry (1 Kings 9:16). Thus Solomon walled and fortified it as an Israelite city, along with Megiddo (just south of Mount Carmel) and Hazor (in northern Galilee) (1 Kings 9:15). However, like Megiddo, Gezer succumbed to Pharaoh Shishak's invasion in 925 BCE. About

> **The Gezer Calendar describes monthly or bi-monthly intervals and gives a duty for each interval, such as harvest, planting, or tending specific crops.**

this time a child inscribed a stone, later found here, with a poem to aid in memorizing the annual agricultural cycle. This has become known as "the Gezer Calendar."

After twenty years of neglect, the excavations were reconvened in 2006, and signs have been placed to identify for the student-observer the salient features of the tel. On its southern side (right of the walking path) are the remains of the middle Bronze Age tower, gate, and water system. Farther along is the Solomonic gate, virtually identical to the ones at Megiddo and Hazor, and a casemate wall (double wall providing dwelling space during peacetime but filled with rocks and debris to provide added protection during war). Up in the center of the tel is the Canaanite shrine contemporary to Abraham's arrival (ca. 1800 BCE), with its ten standing stones, likely representing a covenant among ten Canaanite city-states at this cultic center (*bamah*). The lateral stone with a depression was probably an altar, but it could have been the base of another central stone (*matzebah*). One cannot help but recall Joshua's assembly of similar monoliths at Gilgal and Shechem (Joshua 4:20; 24:25-27).

Bet Shemesh

The name means "House of the Sun (god)," belying its Canaanite origin. In fact, the city sat on the border between Philistine expansion from the west and Israelite settlement from the hill country to the east. Here the cultures clashed, making this an excellent place to read the story of the Philistine capture of the ark of the covenant and its return in 1 Samuel 5–6. Upon its return to the Israelites, the ark remained for twenty years at Kiriath-jearim, which was located on the hill just above nearby Abu Gosh. If you wish to putter among the archaeologists' garbage dumps surrounding the overlook, you will find bichrome (two-colored) potsherds, Philistine in origin. The tel overlooks the Sorek Valley, where Samson's wife, Delilah, was born. If your time allows, there is an amazing natural phenomenon,

Shefela

Sorek Valley from Bet Shemesh

the Soreq Cave (National Park), well worth exploring with the film and guided tour. Down the highway, a bit to the southwest, is the Elah Valley, where the story of David's battle with Goliath is located (1 Samuel 17).

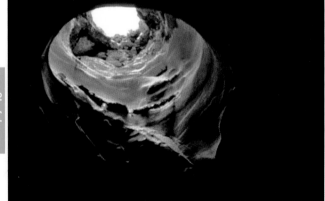

Bell Caves

Shefela

Bet Guvrin-Maresha (National Park)

The only thing biblical here is Tel Maresha, mentioned in the prophet Micah's funeral dirge over Jerusalem's "daughters," the smaller towns lying between the capital and the Via Maris, which were destroyed by Sennacherib during his ascent to besiege "Mother Zion" in 701 BCE (Micah 1:10-16, esp. v. 15).[66] Other than that, there are many interesting things to see, and you need a couple of hours to explore them. It is best to follow the excellent touring map provided by the national park. Given the soft, chalky limestone, many of the institutions are underground dating from the Hellenistic period: columbaria, houses, cisterns and baths, olive presses, and tombs. Most impressive, however, are the so-called "Bell Caves," formed by quarrying (from the top down) during the sixth through tenth centuries CE.

Lachish

The strategic value of Lachish is its location as the major defensive bulwark protecting Jerusalem from invading armies that would inevitably approach from the Via Maris (coastal highway). Micah, however, called it Judah's cardinal sin or "beginning of sin" (1:13) because of its militarism, and, indeed, a multitude of wine

Shefela

Tel Lachish

jar handles were found stamped with the words *l'melekh* (belonging to the king), documenting the profligate lifestyle of the "industrial military complex," which, in Micah's view, was at the expense of his fellow Shefela farmers.

As you approach the city gate, observe the siege ramp built by Sennacherib for the destruction of Lachish during his 701 BCE approach to Jerusalem. The gate itself is composed of two parts, an outer gate and an inner gate, from which you can look to the north to see the double city wall. Both the gate and the double wall are visible in Sennacherib's victory frieze from his capital, Nineveh, a copy of which can be viewed today in Jerusalem's Israel Museum. In the gate were found eighteen ostraca (potsherds used as currier letters), inscribed with Hebrew and dating to Lachish's siege by Sennacherib. The most famous one: "Let my lord know that we are watching over the beacon of Lakhish, according to the signals which my lord gave, for Azekah is not to be seen." Azekah was the neighboring "daughter city," and if she were enveloped in flames, Lachish would be next. Indeed, the prophet Jeremiah tells us that Azekah and Lakhish fell just before Jerusalem was surrounded by Sennacherib's army (for this account, see Isaiah 36–39). Once inside the double gate, peer to the left (north) to view the citadel/palace that would have been the

Olive press

Shefela

final refuge of the aristocracy. Sadly, the local farmers would already have been ravished because the military elite would have locked the city gates.

Neot Kedumim

Neot Kedumim is the Biblical Landscape Reserve in Israel, attempting to resurrect all the biblical flora and to construct models of biblical agriculture such as wine and olive presses, watch towers, and threshing floors (website: www.neot-kedumim.org.il). This is a nice place to have a vegetarian lunch.

Southern Coast, Philistine Plain

Ashkelon (National Park)

Also known as: Ashqelon

Of the five Philistine city-states, Ashdod, Ashkelon, Gaza, Gath, and Ekron, this is the best excavated, and the work goes on. Of most interest to students of the Bible is the Canaanite city gate, outside of which was a shrine where archaeologists discovered the famous bronze calf overlaid with silver with a clay box or "house," now displayed in the Israel Museum. There is also here, in the Roman basilica from the third century CE, a significant display of statues from that period. You can descend to bathe or wade in the Mediterranean Sea. Ashkelon can be visited as the last stop on a Shefela-Philistine Plain day trip from Jerusalem, but it makes for a very long day.

Ashkelon

Jaffa (Old City)

Also known as: Joppa

> **Jonah set sail from Jaffa on his way to Nineveh.**

A great way to conclude your study tour and pilgrimage to the Holy Land is to watch the sun set and have dinner in Jaffa. This was Israel's natural port during the Old Testament period. According to the story, Jonah set sail from here; and according to Acts 10, Peter was staying here when the other disciples sent for his advice on whether or not the Gentile Cornelius could join the Jewish Jesus movement. Peter said yes, and the rest is history.

Park in the Old City parking lot down by the sea. Stroll through the shops and cafés and maybe even buy some art. There are so many other places to explore. Underground is a museum of Jaffa (*Jafo* in Hebrew). Enter St. Peter's Church, originally seventeenth century CE, though the current structure is nineteenth century. As noted above, Jaffa is a great place to have a drink and watch the sun set or, if you have the time and money, even have a full dinner.

Jaffa at sunset

Notes

1. This explains the barren look of nineteenth-century pictures from Israel.

2. *Chronicles of the Land: Archaeology in The Israel Museum Jerusalem*, ed. Michal Dayagi-Mendels and Silvia Rozenberg (Jerusalem: Israel Museum, 2010), 120; picture, 122. The original is in the Israel Museum.

3. Babylonian Talmud, *Megillah 6a*.

4. Josephus, *Antiquities* 18:27.

5. See Lamontte M. Luker, "Herodian Army," *NIDB* 2:812.

6. Greek *tekton*, or artisan, which would be a stonemason; "carpenter" is a mistaken translation.

7. It should be noted that as a fellow rabbi, Jesus had more in common with the Pharisees than with any other sect of first-century CE Judaism, and he regularly engaged them in healthy dialogue. That he criticized some does not mean that he thought all were hypocrites, any more than the criticism of some Christian pastors today implies that all are corrupt.

8. See the section on Bet She'arim for a more thorough discussion of the significance of Judah ha-Nasi.

9. I am well aware of the hermeneutical approach, popular especially during the twentieth century, to view the birth narratives as literary fictions. I find this to be unreasonable. We are not dealing with traditions far removed from their written sources. Luke is a careful historian, in the first-century sense of that word, who received early Palestinian oral traditions including those of eye witnesses (1:1-4). Matthew was especially close to the primitive Jewish Christian community. To be sure, ancient history often included interpretation in the telling of the story, but this is far afield from the notion that the stories have no basis in history. In both this article and the one on Bethlehem, I shall use the sources judiciously.

10. Franciscan Printing Press, *Nazareth*, 2nd ed. (Jerusalem: 1997), 16.

11. A mid-fourth-century CE coin was found, indicating the date before which the church must have been built.

12. Luke and Matthew corroborate the birth of Jesus to the Virgin Mary preceded by an angelic annunciation, in Luke to Mary, in Matthew to Joseph. Both narratives are Hebraic to the core. Though unusual, miraculous births are part and parcel of the Israelite tradition (see Ruth 4:13; l Sam 1:19b-20a; Gen 21:1-2a).

13. 1 Maccabees 9:2.

14. Josephus, *Antiquities* 14:423–426.

15. Josephus, *Life* 311.

16. *Genesis Rabbah* 98:17.

17. *War* 3:516–518.

18. The region is called Batenea and is referred to in the Gospels as a wilderness. This is probably "Bethany (Batenea) beyond the Jordan" where Jesus was baptized (John 1:28). It is also the location of the feeding of the five thousand (Luke 9:10-12).

19. Sometimes in the Gospels when Jesus and the disciples are on the eastern side of the sea, their return to the western shore can also be referred to as "the other side," as is reasonable from that perspective.

20. Thanks to Rami Arav for this insight.

21. "The shrines at the gates" mentioned in 2 Kings 23:8.

22. *War* 7:24.

23. A combined ticket for Banias and Nimrod's Fortress is available, and both are included on the national parks ticket.

24. To view, visit the Golan Heights Archaeological Museum in Katzrin.

25. There are crosses in the mosaic floor, which were forbidden in the Byzantine Empire after 427 CE.

26. See the story of Abimelek in Judges 9.

27. For a more thorough report, see Itzhak Magen, "Gerizim, Mount," *NEAEHL* 2:484–92.

28. See Daniel D. Pioske, "David's Jerusalem: A Sense of Place," *NEA* 76:1 (2013): 4–15.

29. Gabriel Barkay, "Who Was Buried in the Tomb of Pharaoh's Daughter?" *BAR* 39:1 (Jan/Feb 2013): 49.

30. The modern "Tomb of David" on modern "Mount Zion" near the Cenacle is from the Crusades and is certainly bogus. The Crusaders mistakenly thought that Jerusalem hill was Mount Zion (the Temple Mount is biblical Mount Zion), and so they located David's "tomb" there. The biblical books of 1 Kings (2:10) and Nehemiah (3:16) are clear that the Royal Necropolis was in the City of David.

31. See Jeffrey R. Zorn, "Is T1 David's Tomb?" *BAR* 38:6 (Nov/Dec 2012): 44–52, 78.

32. The references to El in the Bible are assumed to refer to the LORD, the God of Moses.

33. Interestingly, it is about forty-five miles, or a three-day journey, from Beersheba where Abraham was.

34. This is Islam's conservative interpretation of the second commandment, "Do not make an idol for yourself—no form whatsoever—of anything in the sky above or on the earth below or in the waters under the earth" (Exodus 20:4).

35. The arch was identified by British explorer Charles Wilson in 1864, and the gate is named after James Barclay, who was an American consul in 1855.

36. The nineteenth-century discoverer, Edward Robinson.

37. Josephus, *War* 4:582. This is a copy; the original is in the Israel Museum. The third word is cut off but referred to the cessation of work on Sabbath and Jewish feast days.

38. Technically it is all the western retaining wall of Herod's Temple that runs all the way under the Muslim Quarter to the northwest corner of the Temple Mount, where the traditional first and second Stations of the Cross on the Via Dolorosa are today.

39. *Mishnah* (Sanhedrin 11:2).

40. This map of the Holy Land is a mosaic on the floor of a church in Madaba, Jordan, which lies between Mount Nebo and Amman.

41. "The second wall started from the gate in the first wall which they called Gennath [=Garden Gate], and [the second wall] enclosing only the northern district of the town, went up as far as Antonia," *War* 5:146. See N. Avigad and H. Geva, "Jerusalem: The First Wall," *NEAEHL* 2:725.

42. In other words, the original fourth-century CE church included this area and more.

43. Antonio Barluzzi (1884–1960), known as the "Architect of the Holy Land," built numerous churches in the Holy Land, including one near the tomb of Lazarus.

44. Mosaic church floor, modern Jordan.

45. The expanded walls can be clearly seen in the model of first-century Jerusalem at the Israel Museum.

46. *War* 7:253.

47. Or simply "in the room."

48. *Epistle* 58.

49. The walls are painted bright colors in the tradition of Byzantine churches. Note how the changing expression of the sheepdog reflects the mood of each scene.

50. Yoram Hazony (*The Philosophy of Hebrew Scripture*, Cambridge and New York: Cambridge University Press, 2012) notes that all the great heroes of the Bible are shepherds, from Abel to Abraham to Jacob to Moses to David. The messianic prophecy from Micah with which this article began continues, "And He shall stand and feed his flock in the strength of the LORD" (v 4a). Luke's birth narrative began with the decree "from Caesar Augustus that all the world should be enrolled." Hazony explains that in the Hebrew Bible, farmers and cities represent the great empires of the world, while "the shepherd stands for people who live outside of society, on the hills" (NPR interview with the author on September 4, 2012). In the accounts of Jesus' birth, Herod and Jerusalem represent the *Pax Augusti*; the shepherds seek the *Pax Christi*. No wonder they are the first to recognize the messiah.

51. *War* 3:399–408.

52. *Antiquities* 17:41-45. In like manner, according to Eusebius, Vespasian tried to exterminate the Davidic line after the fall of Jerusalem in 70 CE.

53. His tomb has finally been found there.

54. Luke and Matthew state that John baptized all up and down the Jordan River, and the Gospel of John probably locates Jesus' baptism in the Jordan River just north of the Sea of Galilee. (See the section on Bethsaida.)

55. Some of the scrolls anticipate both a Davidic and priestly messiah. An excellent resource describing the history of the times, the community, competing theories, and a cave-by-cave accounting of the scrolls is *The Complete World of The Dead Sea Scrolls* by Philip R. Davies, George J. Brooke, and Phillip R. Callaway (London: Thames and Hudson, 2002). See also Peter Flint, *The Dead Sea Scrolls* (Nashville: Abingdon Press, 2013).

56. Duby Tal, Moni Haramati, and Shimon Gibson, *Flights into Biblical Archaeology*, 3rd ed. (Jerusalem: Israel Antiquities Authority [Albatross], 2010), 190.

57. Persons with heart disease should consult their doctors regarding the effects of the salt content and the heat of the mineral baths.

58. Ecologically conscious readers of this book are encouraged to lobby the Israeli government to attend to this crisis.

59. See Lamontte M. Luker, "Rachel's Tomb," *ABD* 5:608–609; *NIDB* 4:725.

60. The Covenant Code (Exodus 20:22–23:33). Contrast Jeroboam's altar at Dan.

61. Though it is possible the basin was for water and cleaning up, analogous to the "yam" or sea in the bronze bowl alongside the altar in Solomon's Jerusalem Temple.

62. These are copies; the originals are in the Israel Museum.

63. See also Emmanuel Anati, "Has Mt. Sinai Been Found"; and Aviram Perevolotsky and Israel Finkelstein "The Southern Sinai Exodus Route in Ecological Perspective," both in *BAR* July/August 1985.

64. There is a parallel phenomenon, much later of course, among the Nabataeans at Petra, who represented their god not with an image, but with a simple rock. Compare Jacob's standing stone at Bethel (Genesis 28:18) and the standing stone instead of an image found in Solomon's Temple at Arad.

65. See Lamontte M. Luker, "Moresheth," *ABD* 4:904–905.

66. Lamontte M. Luker, "Micah," "Micah, Book of," 573–574, and "Zion," 985–986, *MDB*.

NOTES

NOTES

NOTES

NOTES